ALPHABET
ART

ALPHABET ART

With A–Z Animal Art & Fingerplays

by Judy Press

Illustrations by Sue Dennen

Williamson Publishing
Charlotte, Vermont

Library of Congress Cataloging-in-Publication Data

Press, Judy, 1944-
  Alphabet Art: with A-Z animal art & fingerplays / Judy Press
      p.   cm
  Includes index.
  ISBN 1-885593-14-7
    1. Education, Preschool—Activity programs.   2. English language—Alphabet—Study and teaching (Preschool)   3. Creative activities and seat work. I. Title.
    LB1140.35.C74P75 1997
    372.5'5—dc21   97-13762
                                                              CIP

Little Hands® Series Editor: Susan Williamson
Cover design: Trezzo-Braren Studio
Interior design: Chris Hammill Paul
Illustrations: Sue Dennen
Printing: Capital City Press

Williamson Publishing Co.
P.O. Box 185
Charlotte, Vermont 05445
1-800-234-8791

Manufactured in the United States of America

10   9   8   7   6   5

All children ages 2–6 should be supervised when playing. Recommendations for art and craft materials made here assume child no longer puts everything in his or her mouth. Please use substitutions for younger children.

Dedication

To Brian Joseph, Aliza, Debbie, Darren, and Matt, and to children everywhere.

"Each child carries his own blessing into the world."
—Yiddish saying

Acknowledgements

I wish to thank the following people for their support and encouragement in the writing of this book: the Mt. Lebanon Public Library and Judy Sutton, head of children's services; Carol Baicker-McKee, Andrea Perry, Cory Polena, Anne Spero, my husband Allan, my friends, and my parents, Morris and Esther Abraham, and Mildred Press.

This book would not have been possible without the talent and dedication of the following people at Williamson Publishing: Susan and Jack Williamson, Jennifer Ingersoll, Judy Raven, June Roelle, and Jennifer Adkisson.

Williamson Books
by Judy Press

The Little Hands® Art Book

The Big Fun Craft Book

Vroom! Vroom!

Alphabet Art

ALPHABET ART

Table of Contents

ALPHABET CREATURE CRAFTS

FUN FINGERPLAYS!

GREAT ABC GAMES

INDEX

A, B, LOOK AND SEE!

Look around and you can see
things that start with A, B, C.
Acorn, arrow, ant, and air,
button, bubble, boot, and bear.
Check out carousel and creek,
chicken, chin, caboose, and cheek.
Discover D, E, F, and G
and see more alphabetically.
There's dog and dish,
dance and date,
elephant, and even eight.
Find a fish, a friend, a float.
Go get goggles or a goat.

H, I, and J are here to stay,
there's hammer, helmet, heart, and hay.
I is icy, igloo, ill,
J is juicy, Jack and Jill.
K, L, M come easily,
kaleidoscope, kazoo, and key.
L is lovely, llama, lap,
M is movie, mail, and map.
N, O, P are next in line,
notice napkin, note, and nine.
O is ostrich, one, and out.
P's for pepper, pickle, pout.
Q, R, S wait patiently,
there's queen and quiz and quietly.
R's for round and red and row,
S for secret, swim, and show.

T, U, V are on their way
T's tomorrow and today.
U's umbrella and unscrew,
V is vulture, vest, and view.
W is waterfall,
Waffle, walrus, wish, and wall.
The end is here, we're almost through.
There's only X, Y, Z to do.
Xylophone and x-ray help,
Yarn and yawn and yak and yelp,
Yellow, yucca, yo-yo, yew.
Z is zebra, zip, and zoo!

Up until the 1800s, schoolchildren learned to read from a one-page book called a *hornbook*. The alphabet was printed on parchment paper affixed to a wooden paddle and covered with a protective sheet of transparent animal horn. Today the alphabet is colorful and vibrant. It is presented to children on television and in books and is part of a child's everyday experience. My hope is that this book will provide a creative dimension, and at the same time, afford both children and grown-ups the opportunity to share in an active adventure of learning the alphabet.

Here the alphabet engages children in a variety of creative learning experiences. Art materials and techniques are used to craft tactile letters and realistic animals. Non-competitive alphabet games, letter activities, and finger-plays are used to reinforce letter familiarity and make learning fun and exciting.

Each child needs to proceed at his or her own pace when learning the alphabet. Introduce one letter at a time; then, reinforce it throughout the week. For example, you might point out a toothbrush, ten toes, toys, and trees, as words appearing in daily life that begin with the letter **T**. And while you are at it, decorate your home or classroom with **T**s, and **T** sounds.

Recycle art supplies by keeping an art box on hand. Reusing some of the things we normally discard not only helps protect our environment, but also provides opportunities for variation in materials used for projects. If green construction paper is unavailable to craft a newt, perhaps a newt can be made from yellow or red paper. If a child chooses to craft a fish for the letter **F** instead of a frog, applaud his or her creativity.

Always remember to work in a well-ventilated room, assess your young crafter's propensity to put small objects in his or her mouth (choose materials accordingly), and work with nontoxic materials. Remember that younger siblings may pick up odds and ends from the floor or pull items off the table's edge. When scissors are used, please use child safety scissors —never sharp adult scissors. When tracing, use a light source behind the letter, or use a copier machine to reproduce letters directly from this book.

Above all, remember that learning is a creative, personal journey, offering myriad opportunities for shared fun and heaps of praise.

Aliza *went outside to play;*

She climbed atop a giant **A**.

AMAZING APPLE A

Here's what you need

2 large white paper plates

Child safety scissors

Carrot

Poster paint (red)

Marker (black and green)

Here's what you do

1. Trace uppercase **A** on center of one paper plate and lowercase **a** on center of second plate. Outline the letters in black marker; then, cut away the ridged rims of the plates.

2. Ask a grown-up to cut the narrow end of the carrot flat and then cut a notch in the carrot's edge.

3. Dip the cut end of the carrot into red paint; then, press it inside the paper plate **A**s. Allow to dry completely. Use green marker for apple's stems and leaves.

■ When you're riding in a car, look at road signs, billboards, and storefronts. Shout out "**A**" every time you see an uppercase **A**, and whisper softly "**a**" every time you see a lowercase **a**.

■ *Here is a rebus sentence for you to read:

I have new 👟👟. I walk around ☁ so

they don't get wet.

■ Draw the letter **A** on the smooth side of a sheet of sandpaper. Cut it out and glue it on a piece of cardboard, with the rough side of the sandpaper facing out. Close your eyes and "feel" the letter **A**.

■ How many animals can you name that begin with the letter **A**? What about ant, armadillo, and antelope?

* A story described in both words and pictures is called a **rebus.** Subsitute the picture to make the sentence complete.

ape ant airplane Aa

ALL ABOARD THE ALPHABET EXPRESS!

The Alligator

(A Fingerplay)

The alligator snaps his jaws.
Snap, Snap, Snap

(hands together, open and close)

The alligator smacks his tail.
Smack, Smack, Smack

(clap hands on thighs)

The alligator crawls away.
Tap, Tap, Tap!

(stamp feet)

ABC Call-Out Game

The alphabet has 26 letters in it. The first letter is A and the last, or 26th, letter is Z. But, a lot of times, people say ABC when they talk about the alphabet ("Let's learn our ABCs").

Using the letters ABC, play this game. One player calls out a letter like "C" and the others say a word beginning with C, like "candy." Then, that player calls out a letter and on you go until you run out of words. Remember, you can only use the letters ABC in this game.

* ALLAN, THE ALLIGATOR *

Here's what you need

Paper towel tube

Construction paper (green)

Child safety scissors

Markers

Transparent tape

Here's what you do

1. Use markers to draw the alligator's scaly skin on the green construction paper.

2. Cut out green construction paper to cover the tube. Cut out the alligator's tail, eyes, and legs from green construction paper scraps.

skin

tail

eyes

legs

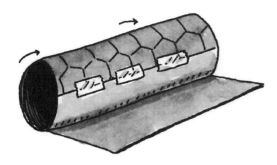

3. Roll green construction paper around the tube and tape to hold. Cut a V-shape in one end of the tube for the alligator's mouth. Use marker to draw the alligator's teeth around the inside edge of the tube.

4. Tape on alligator's tail, eyes (note placement on top of head), and legs.

Meet Allan, the Alligator

▲ An alligator's jaws are set with many sharp teeth. Bite into a slice of soft cheese or a slice of bread to see the imprint of your teeth. Are your teeth as sharp as an alligator's?

▲ Do you know how alligators can see above the water when their body is below the water? Their eyes stick up above their skulls!

BUMPY BUBBLY B

Beth closed her eyes, now she can't see,

And so she **b**umped into a **B**.

Here's what you need

4 large white paper plates

Brown mailing envelope, padded with bubble material

Marker (black)

Child safety scissors

White craft glue

Here's what you do

1. Trace uppercase **B** on two paper plates and lowercase **b** on two plates. Cut away the ridged rims from one uppercase and one lowercase plate.

2. Cut out entire letters from the second set of **B**s.

3. Cut open the envelope and place it flat. Trace the cut-out **B**s onto the bubble side of the envelope; then, cut them out.

4. Glue bubble paper **B**s onto the other paper plate **B**s.

balloon ball book

ALL ABOARD THE ALPHABET EXPRESS!

BARNEY, THE BUTTERFLY

Here's what you need

Clear contact paper

Tissue paper (assorted colors)

Child safety scissors

Pipe cleaner

Here's what you do

1. Tear tissue paper into small pieces and press onto sticky side of contact paper. Then, cover with second sheet of contact paper.

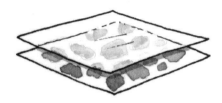

2. Cut contact paper in the shape of a butterfly. Pinch together in the center and wrap the pipe cleaner around it as shown. Bend ends of pipe cleaner for butterfly's antennae.

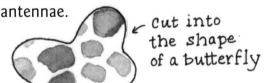

← Cut into the shape of a butterfly

Pinch together → in the center and wrap pipe cleaner around

Meet Barney, the Butterfly

■ Read *The Very Hungry Caterpillar* by Eric Carle. Can you move like a hungry caterpillar? Lie down on your stomach and use your elbows to wiggle back and forth across the floor. How do you move when your caterpillar turns into a butterfly?

■ Try planting a flower garden to attract butterflies to your yard. Flowers such as petunias, daisies, and marigolds are butterfly favorites.

ABC Word Lists

Playing with a partner, see how many **A** words you can think of together. Then, how many **B** words, and last, how many **C** words. Which letter is easiest to use? Which letter wins the game?

◨ In every room of your home or school you can find things that begin with the letter **B**. Do you see a blackboard, bed, book, or ball?

◨ Here is a rebus sentence for you to read:

A 🐛 crawls on the leaves of the 🌳 . One day, it will turn into a « 🦋 » .

◨ How many colors can you name that start with the letter **B**? How about blue and brown?

Carmen drank a **c**up of tea;
She **c**urled into a **c**ozy **C.**

COLORFUL CRAYON C

Here's what you need

2 white paper plates (1 large, 1 small)

Child safety scissors

Crayons (assorted colors, including black)

Toothpick, paper clip, or nail

Here's what you do

1. Trace uppercase **C** on the large plate and lowercase **c** on the small plate. Cut away the ridged rims of the plates.

2. Use many colorful crayons to completely cover the paper plate **C**s; then, color over the colored **C**s with black crayon. Press down hard.

3. Use a toothpick to scratch a design into the black crayon, revealing the bright colors underneath.

car cake clock

ALL ABOARD THE ALPHABET EXPRESS!

◪ Fill a paper bag with cardboard letters. Reach inside with your eyes closed. Can you name a letter you feel without looking?

◪ Here is a rebus sentence for you to read:

The 🐱 is up in the 🌳.

We used a 🪜 to get her down.

◪ Dip the flat end of a stalk of celery into poster paint; then, press it on paper to print the letter **C**. Print a whole lot of **C**s to make some gift wrap.

◪ Ask a grown-up to cut a donut or a bagel in half. Do you see the letter **C**?

My Kitty

(A Fingerplay)

My kitty's tail swishes to and fro.

(bend arm at elbow, wave back and forth)

My kitty sits by a sunny window.

(sit down)

My kitty likes to climb a tree.

(alternate hands moving upward)

My kitty's whiskers tickle me!

(wiggle fingers under chin)

hee
hee
hee

* CARLOS, THE CAT

Here's what you need

2 paper lunch bags

Child safety scissors

Tape, stapler

Newspaper

Marker (black)

Scrap paper (black)

Rubber band

Here's what you do

1. Stuff the bottom of one bag with a small wad of newspaper. Tightly wrap the rubber band around the wad.

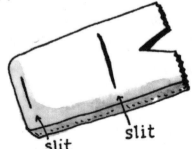

2. Cut a "V" into both sides of the top end of the second bag; then, cut a horizontal slit one third down from the top end on one side. Cut a second slit at the bottom edge of the bag parallel to the first slit.

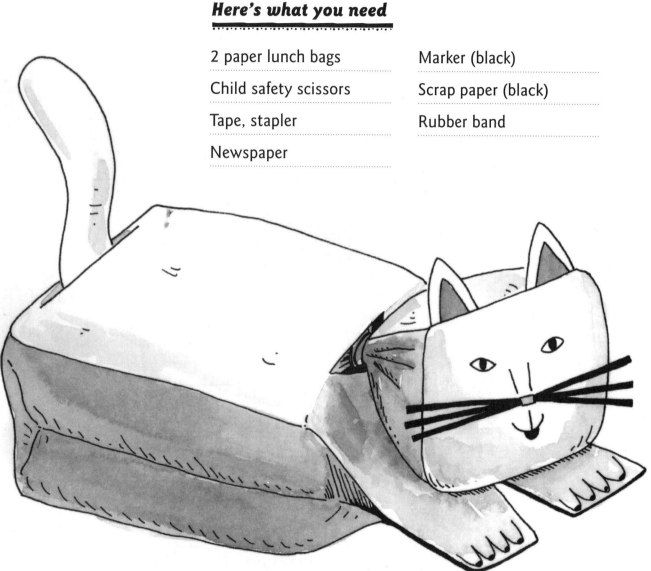

3. Put the first bag into the second through the slit in front. Pass through to the slit in the bottom edge and staple in place.

Staple bag in place

Bag 2

Bag 1

4. Tape the edge of the "V" together for the cat's paws. Use a marker to draw a cat's face. Cut out the cat's ears, tail, and whiskers from black paper and glue on the bag.

glue on tail

glue on ears

draw face & glue on whiskers

glue edges together for paws

Meet Carlos, the Cat

▲ Read *My New Kitten* by Joanna Cole. If you had a new kitten, what would you name it? How about Whiskers or Frisky?

▲ Make up a story about a cat who follows you home from school.

DAZZLING DOT

Deb **d**abbles in photography.
She snapped a shot of **d**azzling **D**.

Here's what you need

2 large white paper plates

Pencil (with eraser)

Poster paint (bright color)

Heavy paper plate

Newspaper

Marker (black)

Here's what you do

1. Trace uppercase **D** on one paper plate and lowercase **d** on the second plate. Outline the letters in marker; then, cut away the ridged rims of the plates.

2. Cover the table with newspaper. Now, pour a thin layer of paint into a heavy paper plate.

3. Dip the eraser into the paint; then, press onto paper plate **D**s for polka-dots.

dog doll door

ALL ABOARD THE ALPHABET EXPRESS!

Dd

✳ DARREN, THE DUCK ✳

Here's what you need

Small white paper plate

Scraps of construction paper (yellow and orange)

Marker or crayon (yellow)

Transparent tape

Child safety scissors

Here's what you do

1. Use marker to color the underside of the paper plate yellow; then, cut the plate in half.

2. Cut out a circle from yellow construction paper for the duck's head and cut out a tail and two wings. Cut out a duck's beak and two webbed feet from the orange construction paper.

head   tail
wings

beak   feet

3. Hold paper plate halves together with the yellow on the outside and tape duck's head and tail in between on opposite ends. Tape plate halves together. Tape a wing to the front and back of the plate. Now, tape on duck's feet and beak.

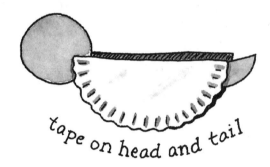

tape on head and tail

tape on wings, feet and beak

Quack!
Quack!
Quack!
(A Fingerplay)

First comes the daddy with his great big feet.

(stamp feet)

Next comes the mommy with her feathers so neat.

(pat hair)

Then comes the babies all in a row.

(walk with hands waving behind back)

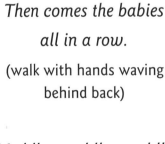

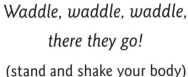

Waddle, waddle, waddle, there they go!

(stand and shake your body)

Meet Darren, the Duck

▲ Imitate a duck's waddle by crouching in a deep knee-bend. Keep your back straight, then move forward, one leg at a time.

▲ Read *Make Way for Ducklings* by Robert McCloskey. Now, draw a picture of the ducklings in the park, trying to cross the busy street.

Alphabet Melodies

What's your favorite song? "Row, Row, Row Your Boat," "Happy Birthday," or "Old MacDonald"? Try singing the melody (tune) of your song, with the letters of the alphabet instead of words. See if anyone can guess the song you are singing. What a nice voice you have!

ALPHABET FUN!

▰ Draw the letter **D** on a sheet of paper. Turn it around and upside-down, until you imagine a picture. Try adding four legs and a tail for a **D** animal. Or, make a funny **D** person by adding arms, legs, and a head.

▰ What jobs do people have that begin with the letter **D**? How about doctor and dancer?

▰ You can surely name lots of words that begin with **D**, but can you name 3 words that end with **D**? Terrific, you did it!

one two three four....

Ed counts each and every **E**.
He finds the **e**nd **e**v**e**ntually.

EASY EGGSHELL E

Here's what you need

2 white paper plates (1 large, 1 small)

Marker

White craft glue

Eggshells (clean and dry)

Waxed paper

Here's what you do

1. Trace uppercase **E** on large plate and lowercase **e** on small plate. Outline the letters in marker; then, cut away the ridged rims of the plates.

2. Place eggshells between two pieces of waxed paper and crush them into small pieces.

3. Cover a small area of each letter with glue; then, glue on the eggshells. Continue gluing eggshells until paper plate **E**s are covered.

Alphabet Ship

Players are seated in a circle. One player starts the game by saying, "My ship is loaded with *apples*," or any word beginning with the letter **A**. The next player says, "My ship is loaded with *bananas*," or something beginning with the letter **B**. Continue the game in sequence through to the end of the alphabet. Any player who cannot think of something beginning with his or her letter says, "Pass."

ALPHABET FUN!

☑ Glue paper punch circles on construction paper in the shape of **E**s.

☑ Here is a rebus sentence for you to read:

Mom bought a new 🚗 . We went for a drive and had a flat 🛞 .

☑ Draw a picture of a newly hatched chick on construction paper; then, glue pieces of eggshell around it.

☑ Gather a collection of small things such as acorns, buttons, bottle caps, pebbles, or seeds. Label the bottoms of muffin tin or egg carton compartments with the letter each item begins with. Then put each in its place.

☑ Read *Bugs and Beasties ABC* by Cheryl Nathan.

The Elephant

(A Fingerplay)

Here comes the elephant,
he moves so slow.
(walk slowly in place)

His long trunk swings
to and fro.
(hands together, swing arms back and forth)

He's so big,
he can't even jump.
(jump in place)

He sits down
with a great big thump!
(sit down)

thump!

ELMO, THE ELEPHANT ✳

Here's what you need

Toilet paper tube

Shirt cardboard

Construction paper (gray)

Stapler

Transparent tape

Marker (black)

Child safety scissors

Here's what you do

1. Cut out elephant's ears and tusks from shirt cardboard. To make the trunk, roll gray construction paper into a narrow tube about 3 1/2 inches (8.5 cm) long. Tape to hold.

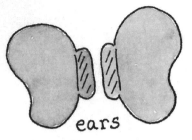
ears

tusks

trunk

2. Ask a grown-up to cut slits inside of tube. Insert elephant ears on sides of toilet paper tube using slits. Staple trunk onto front of tube. Then, tape tusks into place.

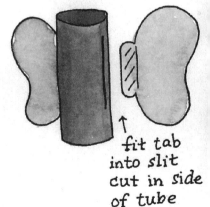
fit tab into slit cut in side of tube

staple trunk on

tape tusks on

3. Use marker to draw on elephant's wrinkles and eyes.

Meet Elmo, the Elephant

▲ An elephant uses its trunk to drink and cool itself. To drink, it sucks water into its trunk; then, it squirts the water into its mouth. You try it — use a drinking straw to suck up water from a glass (don't swallow). Now, move over to a sink and release the water.

Felicia found an **F** that's fat.
She **f**ed it to her **f**urry cat.

FUNNY FLUFFY

Here's what you need

2 large white paper plates

Cotton balls

White craft glue

Marker

Child safety scissors

Here's what you do

1. Trace uppercase **F** on one paper plate and lowercase **f** on the second plate. Outline letters in marker; then, cut away the ridged rims of the plates.

2. Cover a small area of each letter with glue; then press on cotton balls. Continue gluing cotton balls until paper plate **F**s are covered.

Stand Up, Sit Down

Here's a game that will help you "shake the willies out" if you've been sitting still too long. Everyone sits down. One person calls out a letter "**A**." Taking turns, you jump up and say a word beginning with "**A**." Then you call another letter, like "**G**," and sit down. Someone else jumps up and says a word beginning with **G**, like "goldfish," and on you go, "stand up, sit down, go, go, go!"

✳ FREDDY, THE FROG ✳

Here's what you need

Paper lunch bag

Small paper plate

Construction paper (green)

Cardboard egg carton

Child safety scissors

Stapler

Transparent tape

White craft glue

Marker

Here's what you do

1. Cut out frog's arms and legs from green construction paper, and cut two half-circles for frog's eyes. Cut out two egg carton sections.

 legs arms eyes

2. Place bag with bottom flap on top. Fold paper plate in half and staple to flap — round side down — for frog's mouth. For eyes, glue construction paper half-circles on to top of bag, tucking them behind the paper plate. Tape egg carton sections to construction paper half-circles.

staple the folded plate to the bag

3. Glue frog's arms and legs on the front of the bag. Paper legs must be folded over.

glue on arms and legs

4. Use marker to draw on frog's eyes, nose, and smile.

Meet Freddy, the Frog

▲ Cut out large lily pads from green construction paper and place them on the floor. Squat down, grasp your legs just above the ankles, and hop like a frog onto each lily pad.

fox   fun   fork

ALL ABOARD THE ALPHABET EXPRESS!

The Frog

(A Fingerplay)

Hop, hop went the frog
'cross the lily pad.

(crouch down and jump)

"I can hop farther
and I'm so glad."

(continue to hop)

"Croak, Croak," said the frog, on his way,
"you can't catch me today!"

Fill a shallow roasting pan partway with cornmeal. Draw letters in the cornmeal using your finger. If you make a mistake, just smooth the cornmeal and start over again.

Here is a rebus sentence for you to read:

I use a when I go fishing.

One day I caught an old .

I 😊 when I saw it.

Cut an **F** from construction paper; then, place it on the sticky side of contact paper. Cover with a second piece of contact paper. Cut around contact paper for **F** shape. Now, punch holes around the edge of the **F**. Thread yarn through the holes for a sewing card **F**. If you like sewing cards, make them for other letters, too.

Find pictures in old magazines of subjects that start with the letter **F**, such as **food**, **friends**, **flowers**, or **furniture**. Cut them out and glue them on construction paper.

G

Gary *grew* a *giant* **G**.

*He **g**ave it as a **g**ift to me!*

GORGEOUS GIFT WRAP G

Here's what you need

2 large white paper plates

Gift wrap paper

Thin ribbon

White craft glue

Child safety scissors

Marker (black)

Here's what you do

1. Trace uppercase **G** on one paper plate and lowercase **g** on the second plate. Outline letters in marker; then, cut away the ridged rims of the plates.

2. Cut out scraps of gift wrap. Glue gift wrap on the paper plate **G**s, and then glue on bows and ribbons.

girl   goat   ghost   Gg

ALL ABOARD THE ALPHABET EXPRESS!

✳ GERTRUDE, THE GIRAFFE ✳

Here's what you need

Cardboard paper
towel roll

Construction paper
(brown and black)

Glue stick

Transparent tape

Marker (black)

Child safety scissors

Here's what you do

1. Wrap cardboard towel roll in brown construction paper and tape. Cut a slit in the top end of the roll.

↰ wrap

then cut → slit in top

2. Cut out giraffe's head, ears, horns, and mane from brown construction paper. Cut out giraffe's spots from black construction paper.

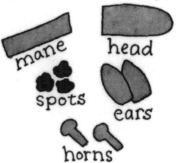

mane

spots

head

ears

horns

3. Slide the giraffe's head into the slit; then, glue on to the roll. Glue on the giraffe's ears and horns. Tape the giraffe's mane to the side of the roll and use scissors to cut fringe. Glue giraffe's spots around the roll.

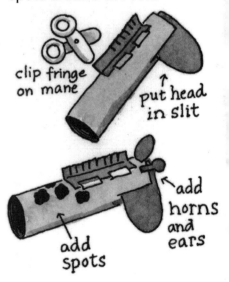

clip fringe on mane

put head in slit

add horns and ears

add spots

4. Use marker to draw on giraffe's eyes and mouth.

Meet Gertrude, the Giraffe

▲ To make giraffe stilts, ask a grown-up to punch holes in opposite sides of the top rims of two large, empty tin cans. Thread a long piece of string through the holes. Hold tight to the strings while you walk tall on the cans. Now you know what a tall giraffe feels like!

▲ The giraffe's neck is so long that to get a drink of water it must spread its legs or bend its front legs or kneel down. Try to touch your nose to the ground while standing up. Do you have to bend your knees?

ALPHABET FUN!

☑ Use your finger to slowly trace invisible letters in the air. Have a friend try and guess which letters they are.

☑ *Look Once, Look Twice* by Janet Marshall uses patterns found in nature to decorate the alphabet. Cut letters of the alphabet from construction paper, and glue on each letter things found in nature like leaves, pebbles, sand, shells, bark, grass, flowers, weeds, seeds, or sticks.

☑ Which words that begin with the letter **G** would you use to describe your best friend? How about giggly and goofy?

Write Right!

One person sits in front of another. The person in back writes a letter on the back of the person in front. The front person has to guess what was written. Then switch places, pick another letter, and write it right!

Hal caught an **H** in the grass.
He showed it to the kids in class.

HORRIBLE HAIRY H

Here's what you need

2 large white paper plates

Yarn (dark color)

White craft glue

Child safety scissors

Marker (black)

Here's what you do

1. Trace the uppercase **H** on one paper plate and lowercase **h** on the second plate. Outline the letters in marker; then, cut away the ridged rims of the plates.

2. Cut yarn into short lengths. Separate the strands from one end of the yarn. Glue yarn onto paper plate **H**s, overlapping strands for hair.

hen hat house

ALL ABOARD THE ALPHABET EXPRESS!

HENRIETTA, THE HUMMINGBIRD

Here's what you need

I paper muffin cup

Shirt cardboard

Scrap construction paper (black)

Recycled aluminum foil

Transparent tape

Crayon (green)

Marker (black)

Child safety scissors

Here's what you do

1. Cut the muffin cup into four quarters. Cut out a small, thin, oval shape from the shirt cardboard.

cut → oval from cardboard

↑ cut muffin cup into 4 quarters

2. Wrap the cardboard oval in foil and tape to hold. Use the green crayon to color the foil.

← wrap oval in foil, then color it green

3. Tape a section of muffin cup on each side of the oval for the hummingbird's wings. Next tape another section to the rear for tail feathers.

add → wings and tail

4. Cut a long, thin beak from the black construction paper and tape onto the hummingbird. Tape small circles cut from black construction paper for the hummingbird's eyes.

↑ add eyes and beak

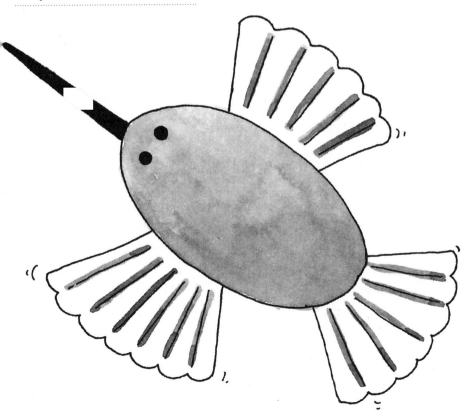

Meet Henrietta, the Hummingbird

▲ Hummingbirds fly in all directions: up, down, backward, sideways — even upside-down. Can you think of an aircraft that can fly like a hummingbird? How about a helicopter?

▲ Hang a special feeder filled with sugar and water to attract hummingbirds to your yard.

▲ Plant brightly colored tube-shaped flowers such as honeysuckle and fuchsia to attract hummingbirds to your garden.

GAMES TO PLAY

One, Two, Three, A, B, C!

Players form a circle around one person who is holding a large, soft ball. Each player in the circle is assigned a letter of the alphabet. The person in the center tosses the ball in the air and calls out one of the letters. The player with that letter rushes in to catch the ball, while all the other players run away. The player who catches the ball then calls out, "One, two, three, A, B, C" and all the players must freeze. The player with the ball gently throws the ball at the player closest to him or her. If the ball hits its mark, that player goes to the center of the circle and the game continues.

◰ Staple together 26 sheets of paper for an alphabet book. Write the letters of the alphabet as you learn them at the top of each page. Use crayons or markers to draw on each page things that start with that page's letter.

◰ Cut out pictures of people smiling from old photographs or magazines. Glue them on poster board and write "A **H**appy Day" across the top.

Isabelle slipped on an **i**cy **I**.
In an **i**nstant she began to cry.

ITCHY INSECT
I

Here's what you need

2 large white paper plates

2 pipe cleaners (brown or black)

White craft glue

Child safety scissors

Marker (brown or black)

Here's what you do

1. Trace the uppercase **I** on one paper plate and the lowercase **i** on the second plate. Outline the letters in marker; then, cut away the ridged rims of the plates.

2. Cut pipe cleaners into tiny pieces; then, pinch together into balls. Glue pipe cleaner balls onto paper plate **I**s.

3. Use marker to draw insect legs around balls of pipe cleaner.

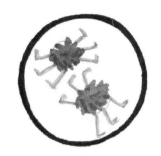

ALPHABET FUN!

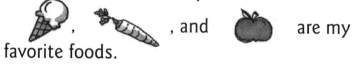 Place a strand of wet spaghetti on construction paper; then, bend it into different letters. Try to make every letter of the alphabet that you know out of spaghetti.

Here is a rebus sentence for you to read:

🍦 , 🥕 , and 🍎 are my favorite foods.

Use a white crayon to write some letters on white construction paper. Brush over the paper with thin, dark poster paint (tempera or watercolor) to reveal all the letters you know.

Read *Ridiculous Rhymes from A to Z* by John Walker. How many words can you think of that rhyme with I? How about my, try, fly, bye, and dry!

Name Games

Think of all the people you know! Wow, playing the Name Game will be fun for you. One person says a name like Bob. The other player must say a word that starts with the same letter, like "Big Bob." Just keep saying a name and adding a word to describe it until you run out of names.

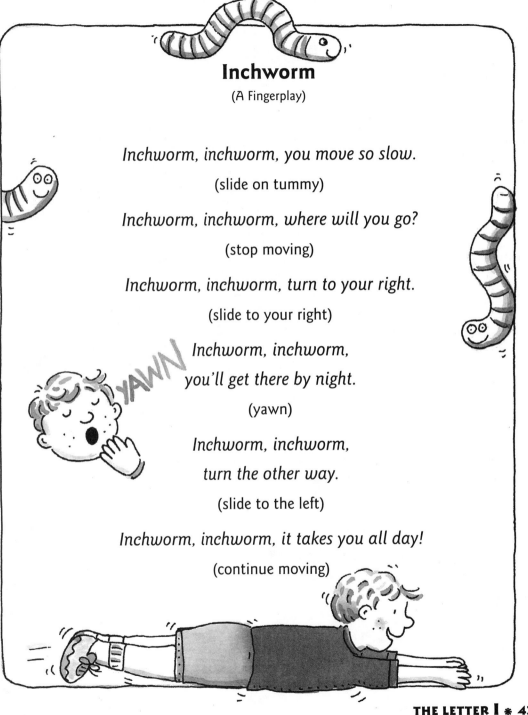

Inchworm

(A Fingerplay)

Inchworm, inchworm, you move so slow.

(slide on tummy)

Inchworm, inchworm, where will you go?

(stop moving)

Inchworm, inchworm, turn to your right.

(slide to your right)

Inchworm, inchworm,
you'll get there by night.

(yawn)

Inchworm, inchworm,
turn the other way.

(slide to the left)

Inchworm, inchworm, it takes you all day!

(continue moving)

ISADORA, THE INCHWORM

Here's what you need

Cardboard paper towel tube

Child safety scissors

Stapler

Pipe cleaner

Marker

Here's what you do

1. Squeeze the paper towel tube flat; then, cut it into four 1 1/2 inch (3.5 cm) sections.

2. Cut three of the sections in half the long way and poke two holes in the top of the whole section.

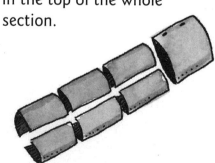

3. For inchworm's body, staple cut sections together end-to-end. Staple whole section on end for inchworm's head.

insect

ivy

ice

I i

ALL ABOARD THE ALPHABET EXPRESS!

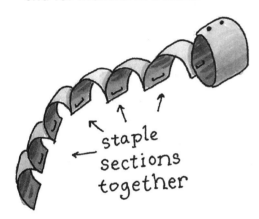

staple
sections
together

4. Use marker to draw inchworm's eyes and mouth on head and put pipe cleaner through holes in top for antennae.

Meet Isadora, the Inchworm

▲ Stand straight against a wall, and ask a friend to use a tape measure to see how tall you are in inchworm inches.

▲ Inchworms move by scrunching up their bodies. Lie on the floor or grass and try to move by scrunching up — no hands or feet, please!

J

*ulius **jogged** beside a **J**.*
*He told **jokes** and ran away.*

JOLLY JEWELED ◈ J ◈

Here's what you need

2 white paper plates
(1 large, 1 small)

Package of sequins

White craft glue

Marker (black)

Here's what you do

1. Trace uppercase **J** on the large plate and lowercase **j** on the small plate. Outline the letters in marker; then, cut away the ridged rims of the plates.

2. Glue sequins on paper plate **J**s.

◩ Do you have a friend named Jane, Jim, or Jared? Their names all begin with **J**. How many other **J** names can you say aloud?

◩ Shine a light on a blank wall. Stand between the wall and the light and make shadow letters on the wall with your fingers.

◩ How many things can you find in your home that are shaped like the letter **J**? How about a candy cane, an umbrella handle, and a coat hook?

◩ Place a long rope on the floor in the shape of a **J**. Try to walk on the **J** without stepping off the rope. Now try walking on other rope letters.

✳ JOSEPH, THE JELLYFISH ✳

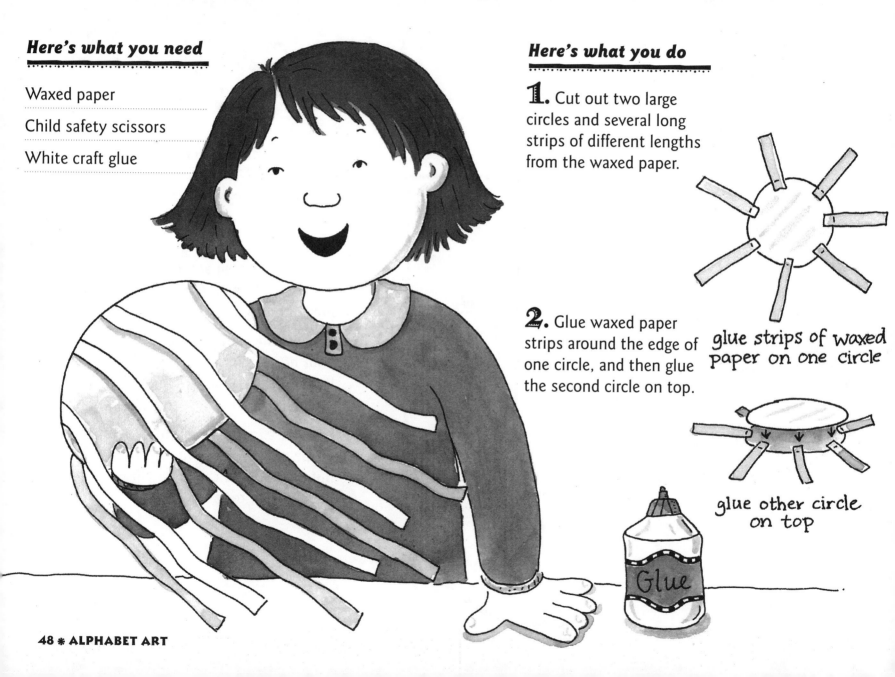

Here's what you need

Waxed paper

Child safety scissors

White craft glue

Here's what you do

1. Cut out two large circles and several long strips of different lengths from the waxed paper.

2. Glue waxed paper strips around the edge of one circle, and then glue the second circle on top.

glue strips of waxed paper on one circle

glue other circle on top

Glue

Meet Joseph, the Jellyfish

▲ A jellyfish has no bones, so its body is very squishy. Fill a cup with a few spoonfuls of jelly; then, close your eyes and feel the jelly. Is it firm or squishy? Where do you think jellyfish got their name?

▲ Jellyfish are so light they float on water. Fill a sink with water and try floating a ping pong ball, a hard-boiled egg, a drinking straw, and a paper plate. Which things float and which sink?

GAMES TO PLAY

Alphabet Roll

Players sit opposite each other. The ball holder calls out the letter A and then rolls the ball to the other player who picks it up, and must immediately call out B before rolling the ball back. The game continues as the players work together to see how far they can get through the alphabet before they miss a letter.

jar

jacket

juggler

Jj

ALL ABOARD THE ALPHABET EXPRESS!

Keisha **k**issed a perfect **K**.
She **k**new that it would be ok*a*y.

KISSING K

Here's what you need

2 large white paper plates

Felt or construction paper (black and red)

White craft glue

Scissors (for grown-up use only)

Marker (black)

Here's what you do

1. Trace the uppercase **K** on one paper plate and the lowercase **k** on the second plate. Outline the letters in black marker; then, cut away the ridged rims of the plates.

2. Ask a grown-up to help cut out an uppercase **K** and a lowercase **k** from black felt. Cut out lips from red felt. Glue black felt **K**s on the paper plate **K**s, and then glue lips on the felt.

kite

king

key

Kk

ALL ABOARD THE ALPHABET EXPRESS!

KATHERINE, THE KANGAROO

Here's what you need

2 small paper plates

Transparent tape

Child safety scissors

Marker (brown)

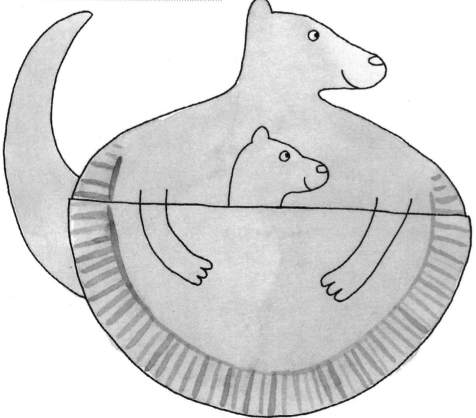

Here's what you do

1. Cut one paper plate in half. Tape one plate half onto the bottom half of the second plate for a pocket, leaving the top edge open.

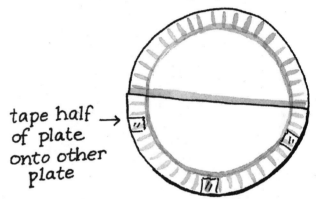

tape half of plate onto other plate →

2. Cut around the top of the paper plate for the mother kangaroo's head.

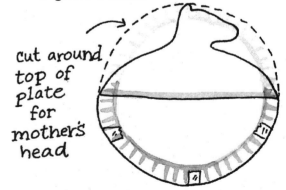

cut around top of plate for mother's head

3. Draw the baby kangaroo and the mother kangaroo's tail on the remaining half plate and cut them out.

cut out mother's tail and baby from remaining half plate.

4. Tape the baby kangaroo inside the pocket. Tape the mother's tail to the back side of the plate. Use brown marker to color the kangaroos.

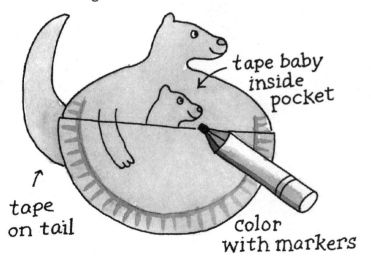

tape baby inside pocket

↑ tape on tail

color with markers

Meet Katherine, the Kangaroo

▲ Hop like a kangaroo across the floor. Try taking a stuffed animal along. How might you hold on to the animal, if you don't use your hands?

▲ Staple half a paper plate on a whole paper plate to make a pocket. Fill the pocket with some pretty things such as dried flowers, note paper, crayons, or stickers.

▲ Read *Katy No-Pocket* by Emmy Payne.

ALPHABET FUN!

▨ How many words can you think of that begin with the sound **K**, as in **k**ite and **k**angaroo? How about **kids**, **key**, and **king**? Try to think of 10 **K** words.

▨ Cut out letters from tissue paper and glue them inside plastic deli container lids. Punch a hole in the top of each lid and hang the lids in a window for letter suncatchers.

▨ To make a placemat, use markers to write letters of the alphabet around the outside edge of a piece of construction paper. Glue pictures in the center of the paper. Now place clear contact paper over the mat. When you use the placemat, try to pick out the letters of the alphabet each picture begins with.

The Kangaroo

(A Fingerplay)

The kangaroo goes hippity-hop

(hop in place)

Then suddenly comes to a stop.

(stand still)

Snug inside a pocket deep,

(rub hand on tummy)

Baby kangaroo is fast asleep!

(rest head on hands)

Lyle likes his Lovely **L**.

He lugged it in for "show and tell."

LOVELY LACY
L

Here's what you need

2 large white paper plates

Paper doily (or lace scraps)

Child safety scissors

White craft glue

Marker

Here's what you do

1. Trace uppercase **L** on one paper plate and lowercase **l** on the second plate. Outline the letters in marker; then, cut away the ridged rims of the plates.

2. Cut out scraps of paper doilies and glue them on the paper plate **L**s.

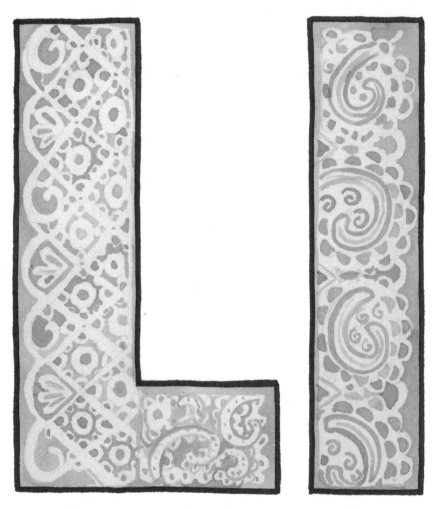

Cut out squares of poster board. Write the letters of the alphabet that you know on each square. Then, punch a hole in the top of each square and put string through each hole. Hang the squares from a wire hanger for a letter mobile. Add to your mobile as you learn new letters.

Here is a rebus sentence for you to read:

I like to read [books] . When I read I wear my [glasses] .

Cut out pictures from old magazines of things that begin with the **L** sound . Look for **lamps**, **lips**, **laundry**, **ladies**, and **lights**. Glue them on poster board for an **L**-sound collage.

lamp
leaf
ladder
Ll

ALL ABOARD THE ALPHABET EXPRESS!

At the Zoo
(A Fingerplay)

I like the zoo,
it's lots of fun.

*Back and forth
without a care.*

(swing arms back and forth)

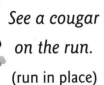

*See a cougar
on the run.*

(run in place)

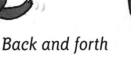

*Elephants
are big and strong.*

(stamp feet)

*Hear a lion
growl and roar.*

(loud roar)

*Long trunks
swinging right along.*

(clasp hands together and swing arms)

*Watch a snake
slide 'cross the floor.*

(lie on tummy and wriggle back and forth)

*I like the zoo,
it's lots of fun.*

*Laugh as chimps
swing in the air.*

(reach arms up in the air)

*Now wave goodbye,
the day is done!*

(wave goodbye)

✳ LARRY, THE LION ✳

Here's what you need

Cardboard paper tube

Construction paper (brown)

Tape

Stapler

Child safety scissors

Marker

Here's what you do

1. Cut a circle from brown construction paper. Use marker to draw lion's face on circle; then, cut fringes all around for the mane. Cut out paws and a tail from construction paper.

2. Wrap a piece of brown construction paper around cardboard paper tube and tape it. Cut four slits around one end of the tube and bend back.

cut four slits around one end of tube

3. Staple lion's paws inside end of tube with slits and lion's tail in opposite end. Staple lion's face onto slits.

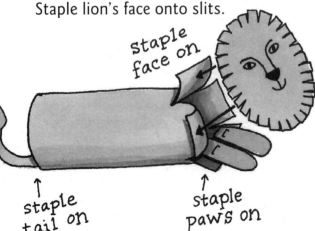

staple face on

↑ staple tail on

↑ staple paws on

Meet Larry, the Lion

▲ To make a lion mask, draw a lion's face on a paper plate; then, cut out the eyes. Glue pieces of brown yarn around the plate. Tie string through holes punched in the side of the plate.

Roar!

GAMES TO PLAY

Alphabet Sounds

Cut out pictures and put in envelope. Now, reach in and pull out a picture. Name the picture and the beginning letter sound, as in **p**umpkin, **p** sound.

MARVELOUS MACARONI

Matthew **m**ade an **M** from clay.

*His **m**other cleaned the **m**ess that day.*

Here's what you need

2 large white paper plates

Macaroni (uncooked)

White craft glue

Child safety scissors

Marker

Here's what you do

1. Trace uppercase **M** on one paper plate and lowercase **m** on the second plate; then, cut away the plates' ridged rims.

2. Outline the letters in marker and glue on the macaroni.

Sound Match

One player starts the game by saying something like, "I'm thinking of something to drink that sounds like the beginning of Monday." The other players guess until one says, "milk." The player with the correct answer goes next. He or she might say something like, "I'm thinking of a color that starts like the sound in boy." The players guess until one might say, "blue."

Players can also play with words that rhyme, such as, "I'm thinking of a word that means something you bounce, and it rhymes with wall." (If you guessed ball, you're right!)

MIGUEL, THE MOUSE

Here's what you need

Index card, 3" x 5" (7.5 x 12.5 cm)

Child safety scissors

Transparent tape

Marker (black)

Here's what you do

1. Cut the index card so it's 3" x 3" (7.5 x 7.5 cm) square; then round off one corner. Cut a long, thin strip from the leftover card for the mouse's tail.

tail   body

2. Bring the sides of the card together to form a cone and tape it. Tape the tail inside the cone. Use a marker to draw the mouse's eyes and nose.

draw eyes and nose

roll to form a cone

tape on tail

ALPHABET FUN!

☑ The next time you go grocery shopping, ask if you can help unload the groceries at home. Put all the **M** groceries in one pile. Look for things such as **mushrooms**, **mayonnaise**, **milk**, and **mustard**. They all start with the **M** sound.

☑ Ask a grown-up to remove the ball from an empty roll-on deodorant bottle. Fill the bottle with poster paint; then, replace the ball and roll letters of the alphabet on paper.

☑ Cut poster board in the shape of a shield. Draw a line down the center of the shield up and down. Now, draw a line across one-half to make three sections. Draw pictures in three of the sections of your favorite things to do. Now, draw your initials in the fourth space for your own personalized shield. Hang on your bedroom wall.

Meet Miguel, the Mouse

▲ Remove the cover from a shoe box and turn it upside-down. Ask a grown-up to cut a small arched opening in the side of the box for a mouse house.

▲ Here is a rebus sentence for you to read:

My 🐱 chased a 🐭. The 🐁 ran away.

▲ Read *Mouse Count* and *Mouse Paint* by Ellen Walsh. Visit a pet store to see mice of different colors. Do you see a black, white, gray, or brown mouse? Do you see baby mice?

ALL ABOARD THE ALPHABET EXPRESS!

Noisy **Nan** began to clap.

She woke **N** up from his **n**ap.

NOODLE NAME

A B **N** C

Here's what you need

2 white paper plates (1 large, 1 small)

Alphabet noodles (uncooked)

Markers

Child safety scissors

White craft glue

Here's what you do

1. Trace uppercase **N** on large paper plate and lowercase **n** on small plate. Outline the letters in marker; then, cut away the ridged rims of the plates.

2. Color the paper plate letters with markers. Sort through the alphabet noodles and put them together to spell your name. Ask a grown-up to help you spell other names. Glue names on paper plate letters.

ANDY
LIZ
JENNY
NICKY
MAX
PAUL
MINDY
MATTHEW
CAITLIN
TIM
JOSHUA
ERIN
ANNIE
SAM
JOEY
MEGAN

nurse nut night

ALL ABOARD THE ALPHABET EXPRESS!

Nn

Here's what you need

Construction paper (green)

Child safety scissors

Tape

Marker

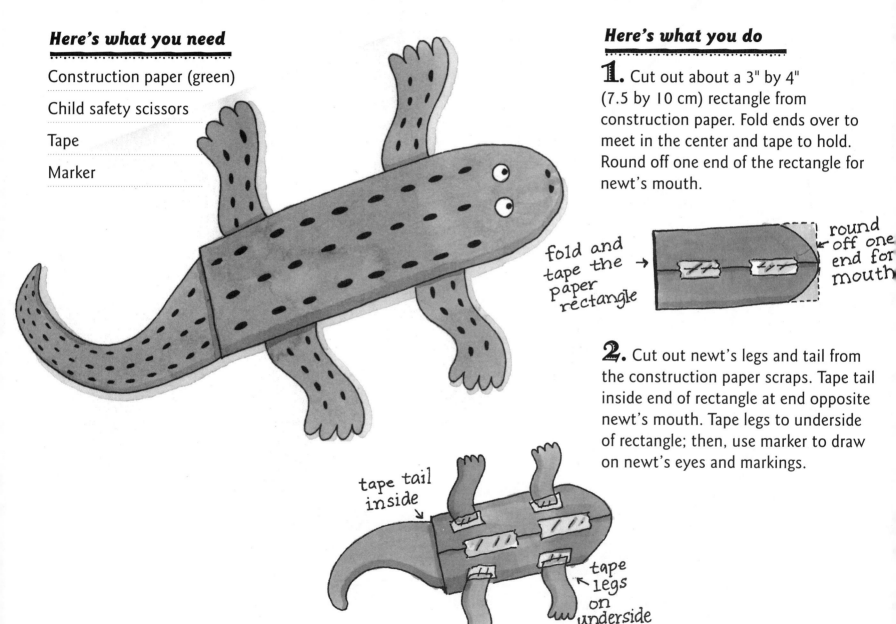

Here's what you do

1. Cut out about a 3" by 4" (7.5 by 10 cm) rectangle from construction paper. Fold ends over to meet in the center and tape to hold. Round off one end of the rectangle for newt's mouth.

fold and tape the paper rectangle →

round off one end for mouth

2. Cut out newt's legs and tail from the construction paper scraps. Tape tail inside end of rectangle at end opposite newt's mouth. Tape legs to underside of rectangle; then, use marker to draw on newt's eyes and markings.

tape tail inside

tape legs on underside

GAMES TO PLAY

Alphabet Bowling

Tape the tops of six 1-quart (946 ml) milk cartons flat. Label each carton with **A, B, C, D,** or **E**. Set the cartons up in a triangle shape: three cartons in the back, two in front of the three, and one in front of the two. Roll a tennis ball and see how many tries it takes you to knock over all the cartons, **A** through **E**.

Meet Natalie, the Newt

▲ Newts are *amphibians*, which means they live in the water and also on the land. Can you name other animals that do this? How about a frog and a salamander?

▲ Newts like to sun themselves on rocks around a pond. Find a flat rock outdoors and put your construction paper newt on top.

☑ After your bath or shower, use your finger to write letters of the alphabet on a steamy bathroom mirror. What happens to the letters when you leave the bathroom door open?

☑ Here is a rebus sentence for you to read:

In art class I drew a ☐ . When I brought it home we hung it up on the ☐ .

☑ Bend pipe cleaners in the shape of upper- and lowercase **N**s. Try bending pipe cleaners in the shape of other letters.

☑ How many names can you think of that start with the sound **N**, as in **N**ed and **N**ancy? How about **Nanette**, **Neil**, **Nicholas**, and **Nathan**?

Ollie **o**ften pushes **O**.
Once it r**o**lled **o**nt**o** his t**o**e.

OODLES OF O

Here's what you need

2 large white paper plates

Round oat cereal

White craft glue

Child safety scissors

Marker

Here's what you do

1. Trace uppercase **O** on one paper plate and lowercase **o** on the second plate. Outline the letters in marker; then, cut away the ridged rims of the plates.

2. Glue round oat cereal onto paper plate **O**s.

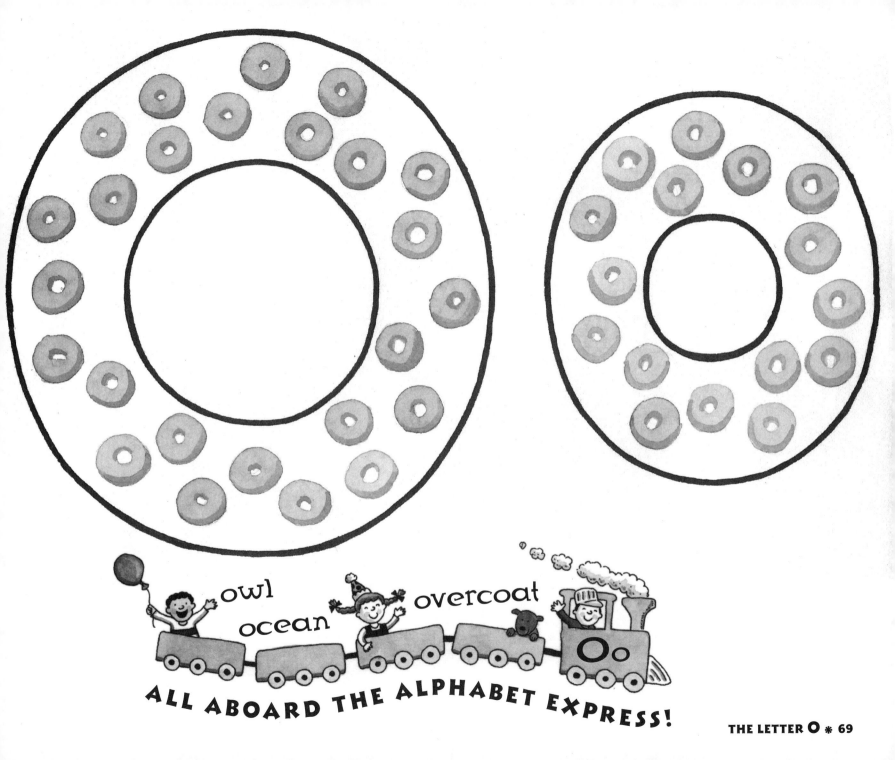

owl

ocean

overcoat

Oo

ALL ABOARD THE ALPHABET EXPRESS!

✳ OCTAVIO, THE OCTOPUS ✳

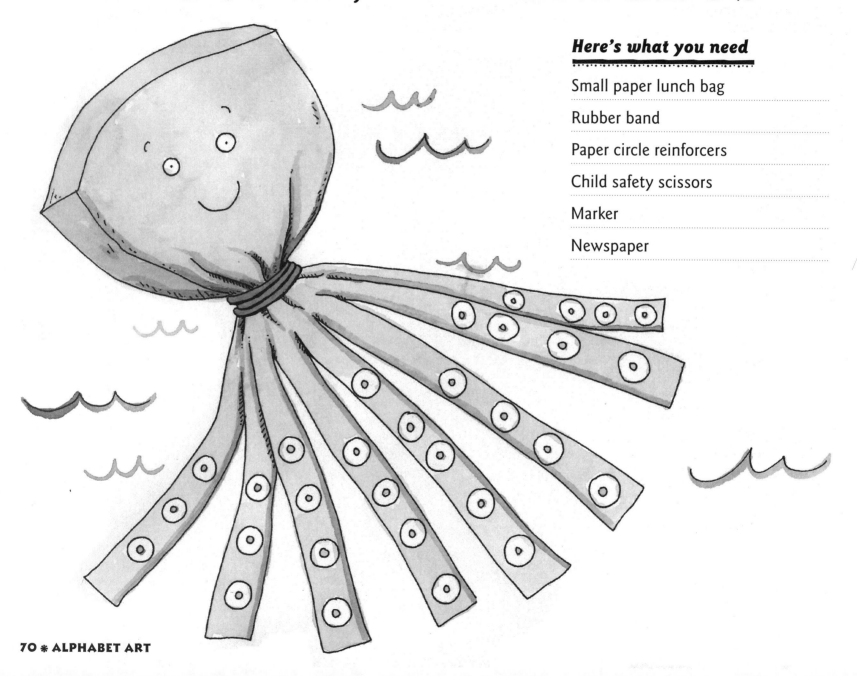

Here's what you need

Small paper lunch bag

Rubber band

Paper circle reinforcers

Child safety scissors

Marker

Newspaper

Here's what you do

1. Stuff the paper bag with a small wad of newspaper. Tightly wrap the rubber band around the bag at the base of the newspaper.

2. Cut up into the bag to make eight strips for octopus tentacles.

cut tentacles

3. Use marker to draw octopus's eyes and mouth on head. Stick reinforcers on tentacles.

draw face

stick on reinforcers

Meet Octavio, the Octopus

▲ Octopuses live on the bottom of the ocean. Fill a clean bottle with one part salad oil and one part water. Add a few drops of blue food color and put the lid back on. Place the bottle on its side and rock it back and forth to see your own ocean waves.

▲ Wrap your arms tightly around a stuffed animal. How many animals could you hug if you had eight arms?

▲ When danger is near, octopuses squirt dark ink so they can escape. Look through a clear glass of water; then, stir in a few drops of black poster paint. Is it harder to see through the glass now?

Here is a rebus sentence for you to read:

I 💗 my 🐶 and my 🐱 .

Hold a paper cup upside-down and dip the bottom rim into a thin layer of poster paint. Press the rim on paper for **O** prints.

Cut out the bottom of a paper cup. Dip the cup in bubble solution and blow big, round bubble **O**s.

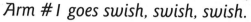

I'm a Little Octopus

(A Fingerplay)

Arm #1 goes swish, swish, swish.

(swing arms back and forth)

Arm #2 helps me catch fish.

(wiggle hand back and forth)

Arm #3 pats my head.

(pat hand on head)

Arm #4 makes sure I'm fed.

(put hand to mouth)

Arm #5 swims me to shore.

(move arms back and
forth in swimming motion)

Arm #6 touches
the ocean floor.

(touch hand to floor)

Arm #7 can grab and tug.

(open and close hand)

But all 8 arms
give me a hug!

(cross arms and hug)

Pam's **p**urse held a **p**retty **P**.
It fit inside **p**erfectly.

PEA GREEN

Here's what you need

2 large white paper plates

Dried green peas

Child safety scissors

White craft glue

Marker

Here's what you do

1. Trace uppercase **P** on one paper plate and lowercase **p** on the second plate. Outline the letters in marker; then, cut away the ridged rims of the plates.

2. Glue peas on your paper plate **P**s.

Please note: If child still places small items in his or her mouth, then substitute pretzels for peas in this activity.

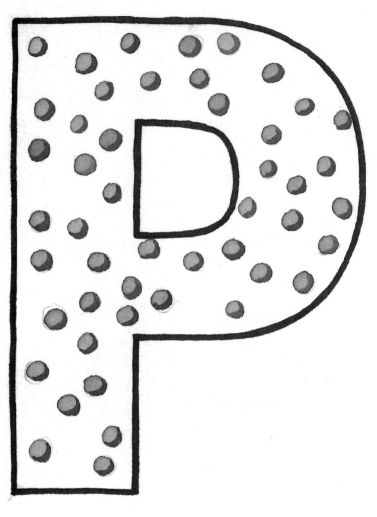
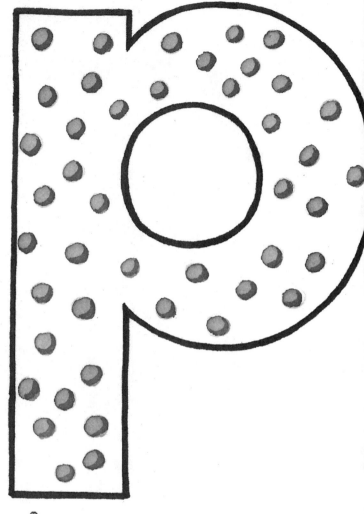

pie

plant

purse

Pp

ALL ABOARD THE ALPHABET EXPRESS!

ALPHABET FUN!

✎ Read *Alphabet City* by Stephan T. Johnson. Take a car ride around your city to see how many letter shapes you can find.

✎ Cut a 4" by 2" (10 cm by 5 cm) rectangle from shirt cardboard. Use a marker to decorate it; then, write your name or initials on it. Cover the cardboard in clear contact paper and tape a safety pin to the back for a name tag.

✎ The sound of the letter **P** is used many times at the beginning of words like **pretty** and **pet**. It is also used a lot in the middle of words like **apple** and **open**. And sometimes, you'll find the **P** sound at the beginning and middle of a word like **peppermint** and **paper**.

Four Little Pigs
(A Fingerplay)

"Oink, Oink," said the first pig,
out in the sun.

(lay on floor)

"Oink, Oink," said the second pig,
"Let's have some fun."

(sit up)

"Oink, Oink," said the third pig,
"What can we play?"

(put hand on side of face)

"Oink, Oink," said the fourth pig,
"We can roll in mud all day!"

(roll over and over)

✳ PRISCILLA, THE PIG ✳

Here's what you need

2 paper bowls (available at supermarket)

Tissue paper (pink)

Scrap of construction paper (pink)

Paintbrush

Stapler, tape

Empty plastic container

White craft glue

Marker

Pipe cleaner (pink) (optional)

Here's what you do

1. Staple paper bowls together rim to rim. Ask a grown-up to cut a slit across the center of one bowl for the pig's mouth.

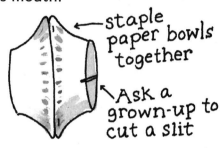

staple paper bowls together

Ask a grown-up to cut a slit

2. Mix glue with a few drops of water in the plastic container. Use paintbrush to glue strips of pink tissue paper over bowls. Allow to dry completely.

glue strips of pink tissue paper over bowls

3. Cut pig's ears from pink construction paper and staple onto pig. Use marker to draw on pig's eyes, nostrils, and mouth. Curl pipe cleaner around a pencil; then, tape onto rear bowl for pig's tail.

staple on ears

draw eyes, nostrils, and mouth

tape on curly pipe cleaner for tail

(Back of pig)

Meet Priscilla, the Pig

▲ Farm animals make lots of different noises. A horse says, "neigh," a cow says, "moo," and a rooster says, "cock-a-doodle-do." What sound does a pig make? What other animal sounds do you know?

▲ Wrap pink construction paper around a can with a removable plastic lid (such as a coffee can). Draw a pig's face on the lid of the can and cut a slit for the pig's mouth large enough for a coin to pass through. Glue ears on the lid and a tail on the opposite end of the can for a piggy bank.

▲ Some animals are used for food. Did you know that pigs give us pork chops and the ham in ham sandwiches?

Quinn **q**uickly caught the **q**uivering **Q**.

It **q**uacked the whole way to the zoo.

QUALITY QUILTED

 **Q**

Here's what you need

2 large white paper plates

Construction paper scraps (assorted colors)

White craft glue

Marker (black)

Child safety scissors

Here's what you do

1. Trace uppercase **Q** on one paper plate and lowercase **q** on the second plate. Cut away the ridged rims of the plates.

2. Cut small squares of construction paper and glue them on the paper plate **q**s for quilt's "fabric."

3. Use marker to make short dashes around squares for "stitches."

Alphabet Memory

You'll need 26 index cards. On the left side of each card, draw an uppercase letter, and on the right side draw the corresponding lowercase letter. Make a card for all 26 letters of the alphabet. Cut each card in half to create 52 puzzle pieces. Place all cards face down. See how many pairs you can match by turning 2 cards over at a time and saying "Big ___" or "Little ___." You can play alone or with others. Always turn your letters back over in the same place. Keep the "matches" to see who has most at end. Then, mix them all up and begin again.

QUENTIN, THE QUAIL

Here's what you need

2 small white paper plates

Child safety scissors

Stapler

Markers

Fold plate in half,

Cut into ridged edge for quail's beak

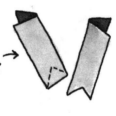

For the feet: Fold rectangles in half; then cut claws.

Staple on the feet & Decorate with markers.

It can stand!

Here's what you do

1. Fold paper plate in half and staple together. Cut into ridged edge for quail's beak.

2. Cut out two 2½" x 1" (6 cm x 2.5 cm) rectangles from second plate for quail's feet. Fold feet in half the long way; then, cut quail's claws.

3. Staple feet inside bottom edge of plate and bend claws back so quail can stand upright. Use markers to decorate quail.

ALPHABET FUN!

✔ Have three "alphabet" meals a day. Start with alphabet cereal for breakfast, have a bowl of alphabet soup for lunch, and eat alphabet pasta for dinner.

✔ Use a pencil to divide a sheet of construction paper into squares. In each square use markers to draw pictures of words that begin with the letter **Q** and say aloud: **queen**, **quarter**, **quicksand**, **quiet**, and **quack**. Draw "stitches" over the dividing lines of the squares for a "**Q**" quilt.

✔ Look at the words quick, queen, quilt, and quack. What do you notice? They all begin with a **Q**, but what else? You're right if you noticed that the letter following **Q** is always **u**. That's always true — **Q** and **u** are always together!

Meet Quentin, the Quail

▲ Quails that live in the western United States have crests at the tops of their heads. Tape a feather to the top of the paper plate quail for a crest.

▲ Some quails are called "bobwhites" because of the sound of their calls. Try to make the sound of a quail by chirping the word "bobwhite" over and over.

▲ Quails don't like to fly too high off the ground. Pretend to be a quail: Squat down and tuck your hands under your armpits. Now hop across the room.

quick
queen
quack
Qq

ALL ABOARD THE ALPHABET EXPRESS!

Ron *remembered to bring the* **R**.
He rode with it in the red car.

RED RIBBED
R

Here's what you need

2 white paper plates (1 large, 1 small)

Corrugated cardboard

Child safety scissors

White craft glue

Markers (red and black)

Here's what you do

1. Trace uppercase **R** on large paper plate and lowercase **r** on small plate. Outline the letters in black marker; then, cut away the ridged rims of the plates.

2. Cut out corrugated cardboard and glue on paper plate **R**s. Use marker to color cardboard red.

road rain ribbon

ALL ABOARD THE ALPHABET EXPRESS!

✳ ROBERTO, THE RABBIT ✳

Here's what you need

2 paper lunch bags (brown or white)

Cotton balls

Child safety scissors

Tape, stapler

Newspaper

Marker (black)

Scrap paper (black and white)

Rubber band

Here's what you do

1. Stuff the bottom of one bag with a small wad of newspaper. Tightly wrap the rubber band around the wad.

2. Cut a "V" into both sides of the top end of the second bag; then, cut a horizontal slit one-third down from the top end on one side. Cut a second slit at the bottom edge of the bag parallel to the first slit.

slit

slit

3. Put the first bag into the second through the slit in front. Pass through to the slit in the bottom edge and staple in place.

Bag 1

Bag 2

4. Tape the edges of the "V" together for the rabbit's paws. Use a marker to draw a rabbit's face. Cut out the rabbit's ears from white construction paper and cut out whiskers from black paper. Now glue on the bag. Glue on cotton balls for rabbit's tail.

tail →

tape on ears

draw face

tape edges together for paws

Meet Roberto, the Rabbit

▲ Cut out a pair of rabbit ears from construction paper. Tape them to a plastic headband or piece of ribbon. Use face paint to draw on a pink bunny nose and whiskers. Now put on your headband ears and hippity-hop like a rabbit.

GAMES TO PLAY

Giant Letters

Using the letters in your name, draw giant letters in sand, snow, leaf piles, or by putting together sticks and twigs. Ask someone if she can read what you wrote.

ALPHABET FUN!

▨ To make alphabet shadow prints, cut out letters from shirt cardboard. Place them on dark-colored construction paper in bright sun (hold letters in place with pebbles so they won't blow away). After 4 or 5 hours, remove the cardboard letters and look at the shadows on the construction paper.

▨ Here is a rebus sentence for you to read: 🥕🥕🥕 grow in our garden. The 🐰 likes to eat them.

▨ Have fun saying the "**R**" sound. What do you say when it's cold outside? "Brrrr!" How does a lion roar? How about "Grrrr!" What noise does your stomach make when you're hungry? How about "Rrrrr!"

▨ How many kinds of food can you think of that begin with the sound R? How about **raspberries**, **raisins**, and **rolls**!

My Little Rabbit
(A Fingerplay)

*I have a little rabbit
who comes to visit me.*

*Hippity, Hoppity
I'm happy as can be.*

(hop in place)

*My little rabbit
eats carrots from our patch.*

*Hippity, Hoppity
the gate now has a latch.*

(stop hopping)

*My little rabbit
doesn't come to visit me.*

*Hippity, Hoppity
I'm sad as I can be!*

(rub hands across eyes)

Sue saw a **s**limy, **s**lippery **S**.
She **s**curried away in great di**str**e**ss**.

Here's what you need

2 white paper plates (1 large, 1 small)

Recycled aluminum foil

White craft glue

Child safety scissors

Marker

Here's what you do

1. Trace uppercase **S** on large paper plate and lowercase **s** on small plate. Outline the letters in marker; then, cut away the ridged rims of the plates.

2. Cut out scraps of aluminum foil and glue on paper plate **S**s.

socks

stamp

school

Ss

ALL ABOARD THE ALPHABET EXPRESS!

ALPHABET FUN!

✒ Read *Animalia* by Graeme Base. How many fish can you name that begin with the letter **S** sound? How about **starfish**, **sea urchin**, **sponge**, **shrimp**, **snail**, and **shark**!

✒ Go fishing for words. Tie a long string with a magnet on the end of a stick. On index cards, draw pictures of **S**-sounding words, such as **socks**, **sweater**, **scarf**, and **seal**. Attach a paper clip to each card and put the cards in a pile. Dangle the magnet over the cards until you "catch" an **S** word.

✒ You'll see lots of words **ending** in **S** because that is the letter used to show "more than one." You have one flower, but many flower**s**, one finger, but many finger**s**, and one toy, but many toy**s**. The letter **S** is a hard-working letter!

✒ Make a batch of alphabet cookies. Squeeze your favorite icing into a letter of the alphabet on top of store-bought or homemade cookies. Can you spell your name with cookies? Eat you creations when you're done!

SALLY, THE SNAKE

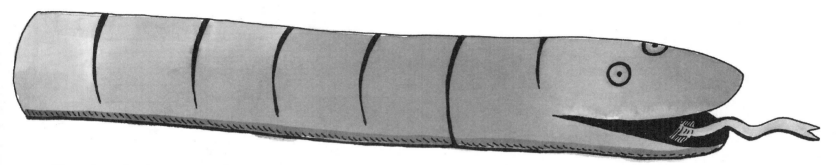

Here's what you need

Cardboard paper towel tube

Cardboard toilet tissue tube

Tape

Child safety scissors

Scrap construction paper (green)

Marker

Here's what you do

1. Partially cut through the paper towel roll, about every 1½" (3.5 cm) for the snake's body. Cut out snake's tongue from green construction paper.

cut slits in paper towel roll

cut out tongue

2. Cut away 1½" (3.5 cm) from the toilet paper roll and round off the end. Tape the snake's tongue inside the rounded end of the roll.

cut a V for mouth and add tongue

3. Slide the toilet paper roll over the first section of the paper towel roll. Gently bend the sections of the roll to curve the snake. Draw on snake's eyes.

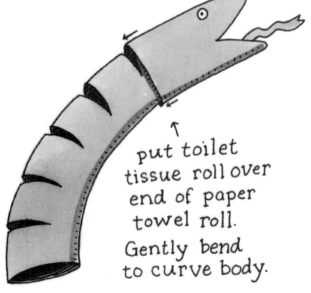

put toilet tissue roll over end of paper towel roll. Gently bend to curve body.

Meet Sally, the Snake

▲ Snakes have no arms or legs. Lie on the ground with your arms and legs close by your sides. Slither back and forth like a snake to get across the room.

▲ A snake smells with its tongue as well as its nose. Try taking a "smell" test. Gather things that have sharp odors, like onions, lemons, pickles, cinnamon, garlic, and coffee. Blindfold your eyes and see how many things you can identify by their smell.

▲ Recite this poem about a snake and then make up your own fingerplay:

Snake
By Andrea Perry

A slithering snake
can be easy to miss,
unless it slides by
with a sinister hiss.
Zig-zagging past
causing fear and distress,
that skin-shedding,
scaly, reptilian "S."

Double Up

The letter "**S**" does a lot of work and it is mighty powerful. Know why? Because an "**S**" at the end of a word can change the meaning from just one to 2 or more.

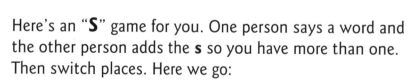

<u>One</u>	<u>2 or more</u>
toy	toy**s**
doll	doll**s**
dinosaur	dinosaur**s**

Here's an "**S**" game for you. One person says a word and the other person adds the **s** so you have more than one. Then switch places. Here we go:

boy   Answer: Boy**s**

Now it's your turn.

hat   Answer: hat**s**

Keep playing; if you need help, ask a grown-up.

Ted told his teacher he needed a **T**.
Since without it he couldn't spell taxi.

TINY TISSUE
T

Here's what you need

2 large white paper plates

Scraps of tissue paper (assorted colors)

White craft glue

Pencil

Marker

Child safety scissors

Here's what you do

1. Trace uppercase **T** on one paper plate and lowercase **t** on the second plate. Outline the letters in marker; then, cut away the ridged rims of the plates.

2. Cut tissue paper into about 1" (2.5 cm) squares. Wrap each square (one at a time) around the eraser end of the pencil until it holds its shape. Now, glue it on the paper plate **T**s. Put tissue close together so that letters are completely covered and look puffy.

Alphabet Treasure Hunt

Go on an alphabet hunt. Write your name on a piece of paper. Take a small bag with you and hunt for words that begin with each letter in your name. If your name is Sam, you might find a soda can for **S**, an apple for **A**, and a marshmallow for **M**. You can find more than one thing for each letter. When you are done, hold up each thing and tell what letter it stands for. Happy hunting!

ALPHABET FUN!

▧ Put a thin sheet of paper on top of cardboard letters you've cut out. Rub a crayon back and forth over the paper for letter rubbings.

▧ Here is a rebus sentence for you to read:

I take a and to the beach.

▧ How many animals can you name that begin with the letter sound **T**? How about **toad**, **tortoise**, **tiger**, and **triceratops**!

▧ "Taste test" foods that begin with the letter sound **T**, such as **tomatoes**, **tortillas**, **tofu**, **tuna**, and **tacos**.

▧ The letter sound **T** is found at the beginning of many words, but it is also found in the middle and end of words. Think of bu**tt**er, ba**t**, flu**tt**er, and no**t**.

▧ There are so many words that rhyme with (sound like) **cat**, ending with the **T** sound. Can you name 5 rhyming words? 10? Wow! Let's see: **hat**, **flat**, . . .

Mr. Turtle

(A Fingerplay)

Mr. Turtle hides his head,
so he cannot see.

(cover eyes with hands)

But if he poked his head out,
he would just see me!

(move hands away from eyes)

THOMAS, THE TURTLE *

Here's what you need

Large white paper plate

Stapler

Child safety scissors

Markers (black and green)

Here's what you do

1. Cut away about 1" (2.5 cm) from the ridged rim of the paper plate. To make the shell, make a single cut from the outside edge of the plate into the center; then, overlap edges and staple together to form a slight peak in the center.

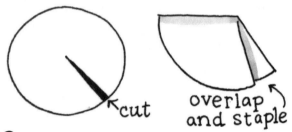

cut

overlap and staple

2. Cut out turtle's tail, head, and legs from paper plate scraps and staple on underside of shell. Use markers to draw turtle's shell pattern, eyes, mouth, and claws.

cut out legs, tail, and head. Staple them on to shell.

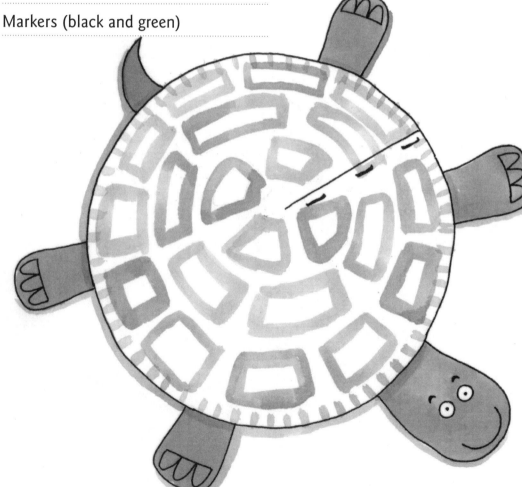

Meet Thomas, the Turtle

▲ Make several paper plate turtles and have a turtle race. Line up the turtles along the edge of a table. Take a deep breath and blow hard under your turtle's shell to move it across the table.

train
tree
table

ALL ABOARD THE ALPHABET EXPRESS!

U

Uri unearthed a buried **U**.

*It was a very **unusual** clue.*

Here's what you need

2 white paper plates (I large, I small)

Child safety scissors

White craft glue

Scrap construction paper (assorted colors)

Marker

Here's what you do

1. Trace uppercase **U** on large paper plate and lowercase **u** on small plate. Outline the letters in marker; then, cut away the ridged rims of the plates.

2. Cut out umbrella shapes from construction paper and glue on paper plate **U**s. Use marker to draw umbrella handles and raindrops.

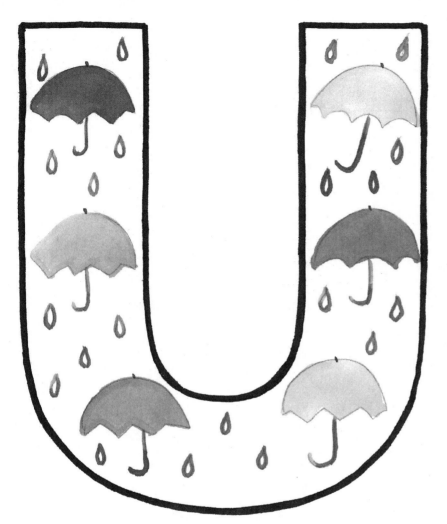

underwear

umbrella

unicorn

ALL ABOARD THE ALPHABET EXPRESS!

UMBERTO, THE UMBRELLABIRD

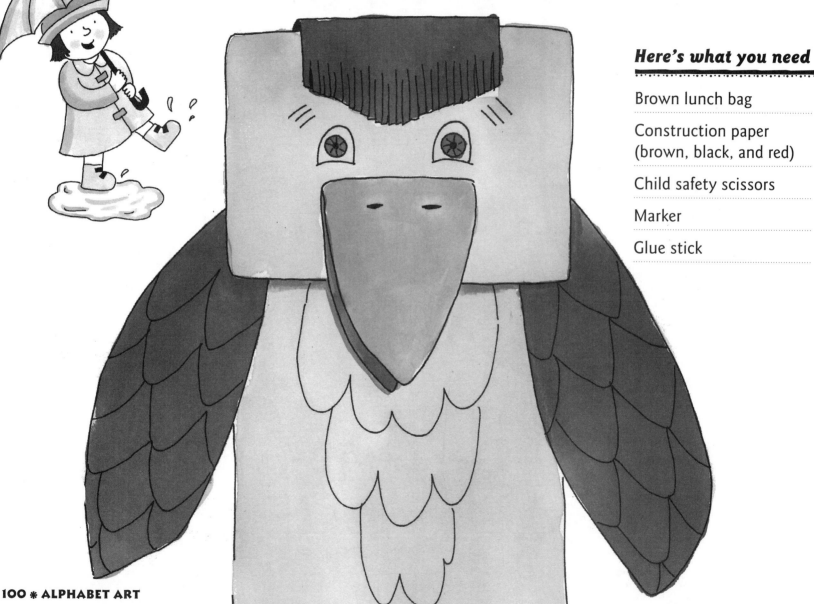

Here's what you need

Brown lunch bag

Construction paper
(brown, black, and red)

Child safety scissors

Marker

Glue stick

Here's what you do

1. Place paper bag flat with bottom flap on top. Cut out umbrellabird's wings and crest from black construction paper and glue on the bag.

glue crest on from behind

bag

glue wings on

2. Fold brown paper in half; then, cut out the umbrellabird's beak. Cut out the red tongue from red paper. Glue the beak on the bag. Glue the tongue inside the beak.

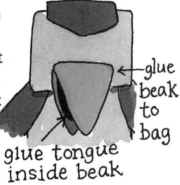

glue beak to bag

glue tongue inside beak

3. Cut fringe on the umbrellabird's crest; then, use markers to draw on feathers and eyes.

cut fringe

draw feathers and eyes

Meet Umberto, the Umbrellabird

▲ The umbrellabird's crest looks like an umbrella. Do you use an umbrella to stay dry on a rainy day? What will happen if you forget your umbrella on a rainy day?

▲ Make up a fingerplay to this funny rainy-day poem:

Pitter-Pat

Pitter-pat, pitter-pat, oh so many hours,

Though rain may keep me in the house,

It's very good for flowers.

ALPHABET FUN!

GAMES TO PLAY

◪ Dip the flat end of a celery stalk in poster paint; then, press on paper for "**U**" prints.

◪ Here is a rebus sentence for you to read:

There are dark 🌥️ in the sky. I will take an ☂️ to school.

◪ Fill a plastic squeeze bottle with water and add a few drops of food coloring. Go outside on a snowy day and write colorful letters in the snow.

◪ Sprinkle birdseed letters on the ground outside. Later in the day, check to see if the birds liked your letters!

What Am I?

Everyone takes a turn. The first person acts out a word without speaking, beginning with "**A**". Others try to guess what the word is. The actor can only say "yes" or "no." Then, the next player acts out a "**B**" word. Play until everyone has a turn as actor.

Vicki **v**anished with a **V**.

*She **v**owed to bring it back by three.*

VINE

Here's what you need

2 white paper plates (1 large, 1 small)

Construction paper (green)

Child safety scissors

White craft glue

Markers (black and green)

Here's what you do

1. Trace uppercase **V** on large paper plate and lowercase **v** on small plate. Outline the letters in green marker; then, cut away the ridged rims of the plates.

2. Use black and green markers to draw vines on paper plate **V**s.

3. Cut out small leaves from green construction paper and glue them on vines.

vest   van   valentine

ALL ABOARD THE ALPHABET EXPRESS!

■ Make the letter **V** with your fingers. Bend down your ring finger, pinky, and thumb while holding apart your pointer and middle fingers.

■ Here is a rebus sentence for you to read:

The dropped its . We  ed them up.

■ Lie on the ground next to a friend. Move your upper bodies apart while your feet touch each other to form the letter **V**.

■ How many fruits and vegetables can you name that grow on vines? How about pumpkins, grapes, and watermelons?

* VARTAN, THE VULTURE *

Here's what you need

2 white paper plates
    (1 large, 1 small)

Cardboard tissue tube

Child safety scissors

Stapler

White craft glue

Markers (brown and black)

Here's what you do

1. To make the vulture's head, fold the small paper plate in half; then, cut along the outside edge to make the vulture's beak. Use a marker to draw the vulture's eyes and nose.

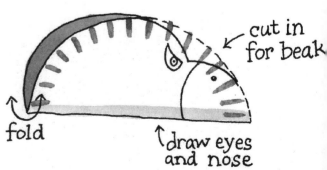

cut in for beak

fold

draw eyes and nose

2. Draw the vulture's claws on the toilet tissue tube.

3. To make the vulture's body, fold the large paper plate in half and staple it, leaving top and bottom open. Slide toilet tissue tube into bottom opening of plate. Slide small paper plate into top opening for vulture's head. Staple head to plate.

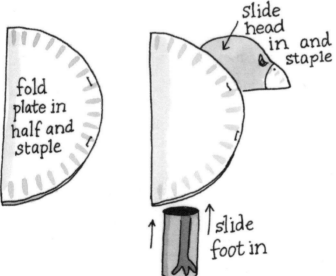

fold plate in half and staple

slide head in and staple

slide foot in

4. Use marker to draw vulture's wings and feathers.

Meet Vartan, the Vulture

▲ The vulture is a very large bird that has a wide wing span. Can you name other birds that are large? How about an eagle and an owl? Can you name very small birds? How about a hummingbird and a sparrow?

▲ Drape a large sheet across your back. Use safety pins to attach the ends of the sheet to each wrist; then, spread your arms and "fly" across the room.

▲ Vultures are known as unfriendly birds. They get their food by eating dead animals. Since the animals are already dead, do you think vultures are really mean? Why?

▲ Read the book, *Aye-Ayes, Bears, and Condors — An ABC of Endangered Animals and Their Babies* by Nancy Twinem. What are some of the things you can do to help endangered animals survive? How about recycling to protect tropical rain forests?

Walt **w**ished **W** **w**ould fit inside.

He **w**ondered **w**hy **W** **w**as so **w**ide.

Here's what you need

2 white paper plates (1 large, 1 small)

Several wire paper clips

Child safety scissors

Marker

Here's what you do

1. Trace uppercase **W** on large paper plate and lowercase **w** on small plate. Outline the letters in marker; then, cut away the ridged rims of the plates.

2. Cut short, horizontal slits in paper plate letters. Attach wire paper clips to slits.

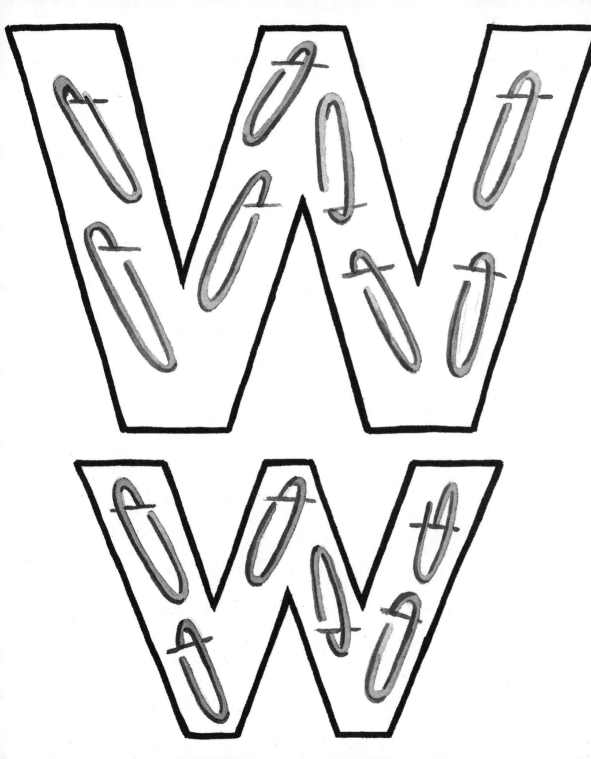

Jumping Jacks

Everyone gets to be a letter of the alphabet. Everyone sits in a circle. One player calls out a letter like "**g**"; all of the **G**s jump up and one says, for example, "**G is for good.**" Now that person quickly calls another letter and all of the **G**s sit down. That letter jumps up and the game continues until the jumping jacks get tired.

WALLY, THE WHALE

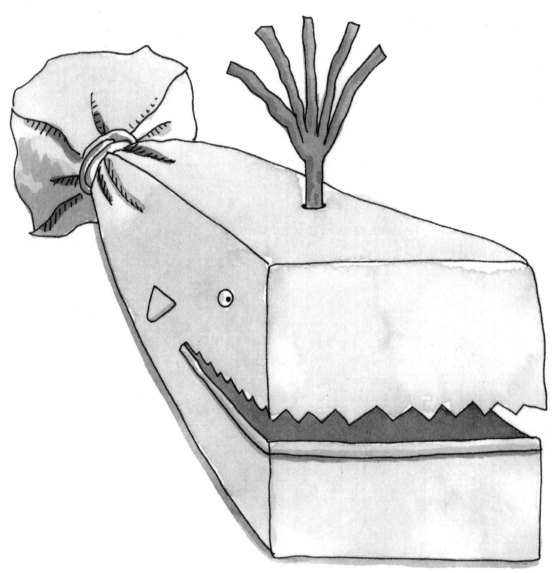

Here's what you need

2 lunch bags

Transparent tape

Child safety scissors

Marker

Here's what you do

1. For the whale's body, open one bag and rest it on its side. Cut into the center of the bag about 2" (5 cm) from the bottom. Cut all the way around, across the bottom, and to the other side for the whale's mouth.

cut slit for whale's mouth

2. Fold down edges of the bag around bottom of mouth; then, cut small zig-zags around upper edge for whale's teeth.

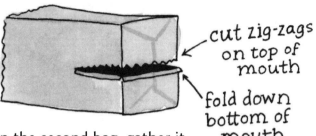

cut zig-zags on top of mouth

fold down bottom of mouth

3. Open the second bag, gather it together, and put tape around 3" (7.5 cm) from the bottom for the whale's tail. Put tail crosswise into the first bag and tape the bags together around the tail.

make blowhole with spray

tape

Put tail into first bag; then, tape bags together.

4. Use marker to draw whale's eyes and fins. Make a spray coming out of the blowhole with foil.

Meet Wally, the Whale

▲ Whales are very large animals. Can you name a very small animal? How about a mouse!

▲ Whales hold their breath underwater but must come to the surface to breathe. Believe it or not, sperm whales can hold their breath for more than 1 hour. Count how many seconds you can hold your breath.

▲ Whales "talk" to each other by making high and low sounds that people cannot hear. Whisper a high and a low sound that no one can hear. Maybe a whale heard you!

Hi!

ALPHABET FUN!

◪ Glue packing styrofoam peanuts in the shape of letters on construction paper.

◪ Here is a rebus sentence for you to read:

At the party we ate 🎂 . The birthday girl blew out the 🕯🕯🕯 on her cake and opened her 🎁🎁

◪ Cut out the first letter of your name from shirt cardboard. Decorate with crayons or poster paints (allow to dry). Punch two holes in the top of the letter and thread through with a long ribbon to make an initial necklace. Try it on!

◪ Make a flannel board by covering shirt cardboard with flannel. Next, tape it on to hold. Now, cut out flannel letters to stick on the flannel board. Can you spell your name?

web
wagon
whale
Ww

ALL ABOARD THE ALPHABET EXPRESS!

X

Xavier's playing tic tac toe.

*Here is where the **X** will go.*

Here's what you need

3 white paper plates (1 large, 2 small)

Construction paper (black)

Poster paint (white)

Pencil with eraser

Thin rectangular-shaped gum eraser

White craft glue

Child safety scissors

Here's what you do

1. Trace uppercase **X** on large paper plate and lowercase **x** on small plate. Cut out an uppercase **X** and a lowercase **x** from black construction paper and glue them on paper plate **X**s. Cut away ridged rims of the plates.

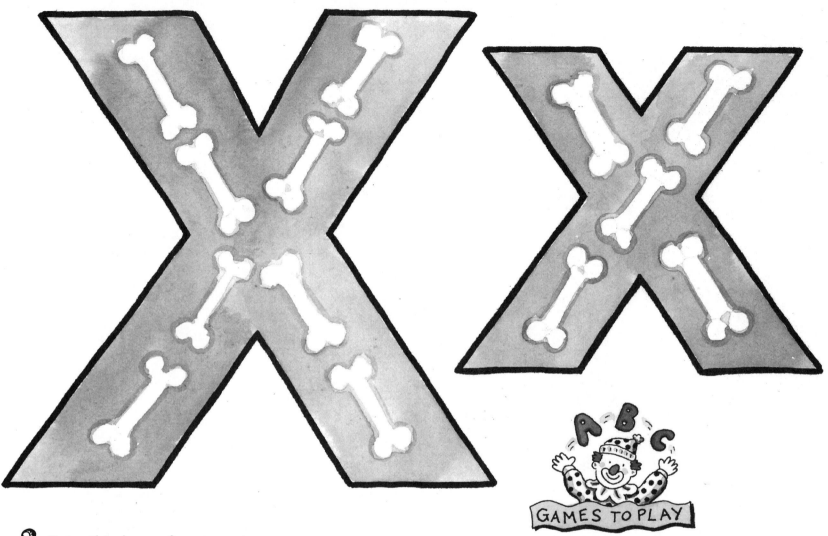

2. Put a thin layer of poster paint on second small plate. Dip the long end of the gum eraser into the paint; then, press on the letters. Dip the eraser end of the pencil into paint; then, press 2 circle prints onto each corner of the long eraser print for bones.

GAMES TO PLAY

Missing Letters

Write the letters of the alphabet on 26 index cards. One player closes his or her eyes. The other player spreads all alphabet index cards face up — except one card. Player 1 opens eyes and must guess which card is missing. Then, switch players, mix up all cards, and remove one card. Play for as long as you like!

ALPHABET FUN!

⬛ Sign a letter with **X**s and **O**s for lots of kisses and hugs.

⬛ Here is a rebus sentence for you to read:

My has a 🌸🌸🌸 garden.

⬛ Spread a glob of finger paint on shiny finger paint paper. Use your finger to trace the letter **X**. Practice tracing other letters in the finger paint.

⬛ **X** is an interesting letter because it is often written with an "**e**" before it. **X** (like in **x**-ray) is the sound in **extra**, **excellent**, and **excite**. Do you notice the **e** before the **x**?

Little Fish
(A Fingerplay)

Nibble, nibble on my line.

(move hand up and down)

Little fish, will you be mine?

(shake head back and forth)

Reel it up and see it grin,

(move hand round and round)

Then throw that little fish back in!

(make throwing motion)

XENIA, THE X-RAY FISH

Here's what you need

Two sheets waxed paper

Aluminum foil

White craft glue

Child safety scissors

Newspaper

Iron (for grown-up use only)

Here's what you do

1. Place one sheet of waxed paper on top of another; then, cut out a fish. Separate the two waxed paper fish. Cut aluminum foil into strips for fish bones. Glue foil fish bones on one waxed paper fish. Now, cover with the second fish.

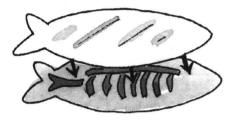

2. Place waxed paper fish between newspaper. Ask a grown-up to iron quickly back and forth over the fish to hold waxed paper together.

Meet Xenia, the X-Ray Fish

▲ Cut out a fish tank from blue construction paper. Glue on fish snack crackers (or fish from old magazines). Now, use marker to decorate the tank with grass, gravel, and a sunken treasure chest.

▲ Visit an aquarium (or a pet store) to see many different kinds of fish. Do they have an X-ray fish? Look for other see-through fish in the aquarium. Are they big or small?

ALL ABOARD THE ALPHABET EXPRESS!

Yasmine **y**anked a **y**ellow **Y**.

*She baked it in a **y**ummy pie.*

YELLOW YARN
Y

Here's what you need

2 large white paper plates

Yarn (yellow)

Child safety scissors

White craft glue

Here's what you do

1. Trace uppercase **Y** on one paper plate and lowercase **y** on second plate. Outline the letters in marker; then, cut away the ridged rims of the plates.

2. Cut yarn into short strips and glue on paper plate **Y**s.

YOLANDA, THE YAK ✳

Here's what you need

Brown paper lunch bag

Construction paper (brown)

Marker (black)

Glue stick

Child safety scissors

Here's what you do

1. Place paper bag flat with bottom flap on top. Cut out yak's face, ears, and horns from brown construction paper. Glue ears on sides of bag, horns on top, and face below the flap.

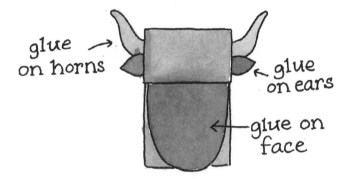

glue on horns →

← glue on ears

← glue on face

2. Cut out yak's hair from brown construction paper and glue across top flap of bag. Use scissors to fringe yak's hair and beard. Use markers to draw yak's eyes, nose, and mouth.

glue on hair, then cut fringe

draw face

cut fringe

Meet Yolanda, the Yak

▲ Yaks climb on steep rocks. Scatter some old pillows and chair cushions on the floor. Pretend they are rocks and climb across them without stepping on the floor.

▲ Yaks carry their heads so low their noses almost touch the ground. How low do you have to bend to touch your nose to the ground? Can you walk that way?

ALPHABET FUN!

GAMES TO PLAY

Alphabet Rhyme Time

One player says a word that starts with the letter **A**, such as **art**. The next player must then say a word that rhymes with **art**, such as **start**. Play continues until a player cannot think of a rhyming word. Then, start a new round by saying a word that begins with the next letter of the alphabet, such as **ball**. Players must then take turns saying words that rhyme with **ball,** such as **fall**.

◪ Glue yarn on shirt cardboard in the shapes of different letters.

◪ Paint a "**y**ellow" picture. You might want to include a lemon, a duck, a school bus, and the sun.

◪ Here is a rebus sentence for you to read:

Playing 🏐 , eating 🍦 , and reading 📖s, are three of my favorite things to do.

yarn   yawn   yard

ALL ABOARD THE ALPHABET EXPRESS!

MAKE A ZIG-ZAG

Here's what you need

2 large white paper plates

Black tape

Marker (black)

Child safety scissors

Here's what you do

1. Trace uppercase **Z** on one paper plate and lowercase **z** on second plate. Outline the letters in marker; then, cut away the ridged rims of the plates.

2. Cut black tape (or use black marker) into short thin strips and glue on paper plate **Z**s.

Zoe drew a **z**ig-**z**ag **Z**.

It zoomed away impatiently.

zoo

zero

zipper

ALL ABOARD THE ALPHABET EXPRESS!

Alphabet Parade

◪ Have a zig-zag race outdoors. Draw a long zig-zag line with chalk on a sidewalk or driveway. Each racer must stay on the line and can run, walk, hop, or skip to the end.

◪ Read *The Graphic Alphabet* by David Pelletier. Tear construction paper in the shapes of letters and glue the letters on poster board for a torn-paper alphabet.

◪ Use a computer or typewriter to type rows of **ZZZZZZZZZZZZZZZZ**s. Cut out the rows of **z**s and glue them on paper to make "**Z**" designs.

◪ How many words beginning or ending with the **z** sound (like in **z**ebra or bu**zz**) can you say aloud?

Gather your friends together for an alphabet parade. Each person picks 2 letters and prints them very large on pieces of paper. Tape one letter to your chest and one on your back. Now make some sound toys (pots, pans, spoons, comb kazoos, nut maracas), get in line, and march to the alphabet song ("A B C D E F G, H I J K L M N O P, Q R S, T U V, W X, Y and Z. Now I know my ABCs, next time won't you play with me?"). At anytime the leader can call, "Switch," and everyone marches backward. Then the leader calls, "Switch" again and you march forward. Play until you are tired.

ZELDA, THE ZEBRA

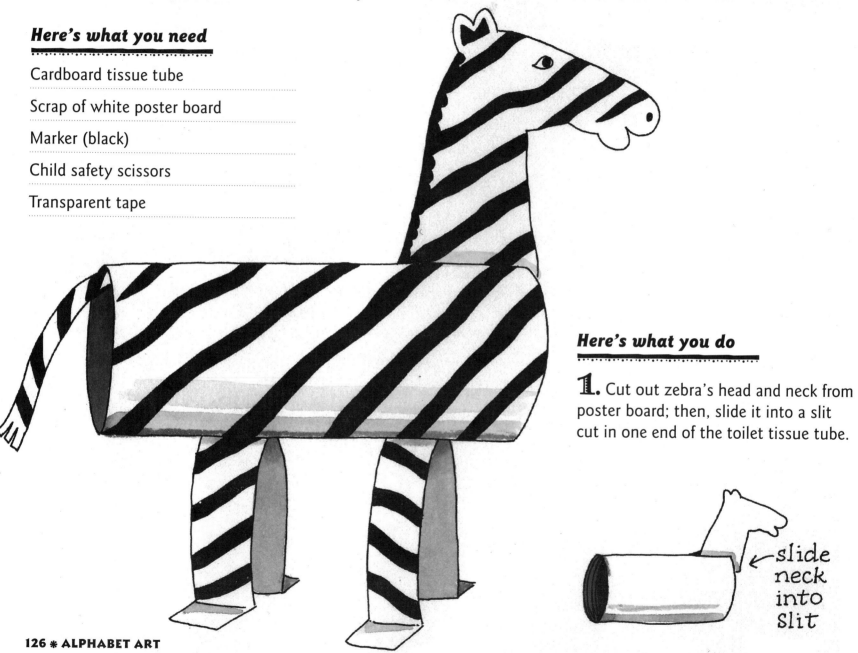

Here's what you need

Cardboard tissue tube

Scrap of white poster board

Marker (black)

Child safety scissors

Transparent tape

Here's what you do

1. Cut out zebra's head and neck from poster board; then, slide it into a slit cut in one end of the toilet tissue tube.

slide neck into slit

2. Ask a grown-up to help you cut four crosswise slits parallel to each other in the bottom of the tube. Cut out two strips of poster board about 6" x ¾" (15 cm x 2 cm) for zebra's legs. Thread each leg through one slit and out the other. Bend back the ends of the legs so zebra can stand upright.

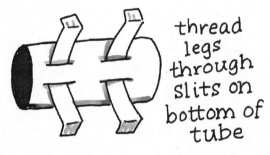

thread legs through slits on bottom of tube

3. Cut tail from poster board and use scissors to make fringe. Tape tail inside tube. Use marker to draw stripes on zebra.

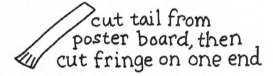

cut tail from poster board, then cut fringe on one end

tape tail inside tube

draw stripes with marker

Meet Zelda, the Zebra

▲ No two zebras have identical stripes, just like no two people have identical fingerprints. Press a finger on an ink pad; then, press it on paper to see your fingerprint. Have a friend do the same and then compare the prints. Even each one of your own fingerprints is different — compare all ten!

▲ How many things can you see that are black and white? How about white snow falling from a black nighttime sky? How about newspaper, with black print on white paper?

INDEX

Activities

alphabet book, 40
alphabet cookies, 89
alphabet meals, 81
alphabet singing, 22, 125
aquarium and pet store, 63, 117
bird names, 107
birdseed letters, 102
black and white objects, 127
blowing bubbles, 72
body letter, 105
in the car, 4, 75
draw a picture, 22
fingerprints, comparing, 127
fishing for words, 89
fish names, 89
food letter, 15
grocery names, 63
holding breath, 111
hummingbird feeder, 40
inchworm inches, 45
kinds of food, 86
letter picture, 22
letter rubbings, 95
letters in the snow, 102
letter sounds, 86
naming colors, 12
naming friends, 47, 67
newt on a rock, 67
object labeling, 25
paper plate turtle race, 97
prints, shadow, 86
rope letters, 47
"s" game, 92
spaghetti letters, 42
story, create a, 17

whispering, 111
wings from a sheet, 107
word descriptions, 36
word quilt, 81
Xs and Os, 115
"yellow" picture, 122
"zzzzz" designs, 125
See also **Crafts; Games**

Animals

alligators, 6-7
bird names, 107
butterflies, 10-11
cats, 16-17
ducks, 20-22
elephants, 26-27
endangered, 107
fish, 116-117
food from, 77
frogs, 30-31
giraffes, 35-36
hummingbirds, 39-40
inchworms, 44-45
jellyfish, 48-49
kangaroos, 52-53
lions, 58-59
mice, 62-63
naming, 4, 95, 107, 111
newts, 66-67
octopuses, 70-71
pigs, 76-77
quails, 80-81
rabbits, 84-85
snakes, 90-91
sounds of, 77, 81
turtles, 96-97
umbrellabirds, 100-101

vultures, 106-107
whales, 110-111
yaks, 120-121
zebras, 126-127

Books

Alphabet City, 75
Animalia, 89
Aye-Ayes, Bears, and Condors-An ABC of Endangered Animals and Their Babies, 107
Bugs and Beasties ABC, 25
Graphic Alphabet, The, 125
Katy No-Pocket, 53
Look Once, Look Twice, 36
Make Way for Ducklings, 22
Mouse Count, 63
Mouse Paint, 63
My New Kitten, 17
Ridiculous Rhymes from A to Z, 42
Very Hungry Caterpillar, The, 11

Compare/contrast

alligator teeth, 7
birds, 107
fingerprints, 127
fish, 117
hummingbirds, 40
letter J, 47
octopuses, 71
whales, 111

Crafts

alligator, cardboard tube, 6-7
alphabet book, create an, 40
alphabet noodle name, 64
aluminum foil letter, 87
apple, painting a paper, 2
bubble paper letter, 8
butterfly, tissue paper, 10-11

Little Hands® Books from Williamson Publishing

The following *Little Hands*® books for ages 2 to 6 are each 144 pages, fully illustrated, trade paper, 10 x 8, $12.95 US. To order additional copies of *Alphabet Art* or any other books, please see last page for ordering information. Thank you.

Children's BOMC Main Selection

THE LITTLE HANDS® ART BOOK

Exploring Arts & Crafts with 2- to 6-Year-Olds

by Judy Press

Parents' Choice Approved

THE LITTLE HANDS®
BIG FUN CRAFT BOOK

Creative Fun for 2- to 6-Year-Olds

by Judy Press

MATH PLAY!

80 Ways to Count & Learn

by Diane McGowan and Mark Schrooten

FUN WITH MY 5 SENSES

Activities to Build Learning Readiness

by Sarah A. Williamson

Parents' Choice Approved

THE LITTLE HANDS® NATURE BOOK

Earth, Sky, Critters & More

by Nancy Fusco Castaldo

Parents' Choice Approved
Early Childhood News Directors' Choice Award

SHAPES, SIZES & MORE SURPRISES!

A Little Hands® Early Learning Book

by Mary Tomczyk

American Bookseller Pick of the Lists

RAINY DAY PLAY!

Explore, Create, Discover, Pretend

by Nancy Fusco Castaldo

Kids Can!® Books from Williamson Publishing

The following *Kids Can!* ® books for ages 4 to 10 are each 160-176 pages, fully illustrated, trade paper, 11 x 8 1/2, $12.95 US.

Early Childhood News Directors' Choice Award

VROOM! VROOM!
Making 'dozers, 'copters, trucks & more
by Judy Press

Oppenheim Toy Best Book Award
Benjamin Franklin Best Nonfiction Book Award
American Bookseller Pick of the Lists

SUPER SCIENCE CONCOCTIONS
50 Mysterious Mixtures for Fabulous Fun
by Jill Frankel Hauser

Benjamin Franklin Best Multicultural Book Award
Parents' Choice Approved
Skipping Stones Multicultural Honor Award

THE KIDS' MULTICULTURAL COOKBOOK
Food & Fun Around the World
by Deanna F. Cook

Oppenheim Toy Portfolio Best Book Award
American Bookseller Pick of the Lists

THE KIDS' SCIENCE BOOK
Creative Experiences for Hands-On Fun
by Robert Hirschfeld and Nancy White

Parents' Choice Gold Award
American Bookseller Pick of the Lists
Oppenheim Toy Portfolio Best Book Award

THE KIDS' MULTICULTURAL ART BOOK
Art & Craft Experiences from Around the World
by Alexandra M. Terzian

BOREDOM BUSTERS!
The Curious Kids' Activity Book
by Avery Hart & Paul Mantell

Parents' Choice Gold Award Winner
Parents Magazine Parents' Pick

THE KIDS' NATURE BOOK (NEWLY REVISED)
365 Indoor/Outdoor Activities and Experiences
by Susan Milord

Parents' Choice Approved
Dr. Toy Vacation Favorites Award

KIDS GARDEN!
The Anytime, Anyplace Guide to Sowing & Growing Fun
by Avery Hart and Paul Mantell

Other Books From Williamson Publishing

American Bookseller Pick of the Lists

PYRAMIDS!

50 Hands-On Activities to Experience Ancient Egypt
by Avery Hart & Paul Mantell
96 pages, 10 x 10
Trade paper, $10.95

Benjamin Franklin Best Juvenile Fiction Award
Parents' Choice Honor Award
Stepping Stones Multicultural Honor Award

TALES ALIVE!

Ten Multicultural Folktales with Activities
by Susan Milord
128 pages, 8 1/2 x 11
Trade paper, $15.95

Benjamin Franklin Best Juvenile Fiction Award
Benjamin Franklin Best Multicultural Award
Parents' Choice Approved

TALES OF THE SHIMMERING SKY

Ten Global Folktales with Activities
by Susan Milord
128 pages, 8 1/2 x 11
Trade paper, $15.95

To see what's new at Williamson and learn more about specific books, visit our website at:

http://www.williamsonbooks.com

To Order Books:

You'll find Williamson books at your favorite bookstore or order directly from Williamson Publishing. We accept Visa and MasterCard *(please include the number and expiration date)*, or send check to:

Williamson Publishing Company
Church Hill Road, P.O. Box 185
Charlotte, Vermont 05445

Toll-free phone orders with credit cards:
1-800-234-8791   Extension 0

E-mail orders with credit cards:
order@williamsonbooks.com
Catalog request: **mail, phone, or e-mail**

Please add **$3.20** for postage for one book plus **50 cents** for each additional book. Satisfaction is guaranteed or full refund without questions or quibbles.

Prices may be slightly higher when purchased in Canada.

Kids Can!®, *Little Hands*®, and *Tales Alive!*® are registered trademarks of Williamson Publishing. *Kaleidoscope Kids*™ is a trademark of Williamson Publishing.